Animals, Houses & People

Craig Hinshaw

Be Bold!
Craig Hinshaw

Poodles Press 2013

"Craig Hinshaw has done it again! First with his "Clay Connections," and now with his inspiring (and fun) ***"Animals, Houses & People."*** *Elementary teachers would do well to pick up this book and make use of Craig's hands'on advice, practical tips and lesson plans — both basic and "extreme."*

Maryellen Bridge
Editor and Publisher,
Arts and Activities Magazine

"Early childhood art goes to the extremes in Craig Hinshaw's new book, ***Animals, Houses and People.*** *Hinshaw's engaging interdisciplinary lessons set high expectations as he never underestimates their ideas and abilities of his young students. He knows how to plant and nurture the seed of imagination and shares it here."*

Nancy Walkup
Editor, School Arts Magazine
NAEA Elementary Director

"Once again Craig has shown that art lessons for children do not have to be overly complex. ***Animals, Houses & People*** *will be a regular resource for any busy art teacher."*

Dennis Inhulsen
NAEA President

To Sara and Alison

Special Thanks to:

Carol whose encouragement, support and insightful proof-reading made this book possible.

All the Lamphere elementary classroom teachers and principals that enthusiastically supported and became part of the extreme art lessons.

The wonderful Lamphere custodians who smilingly tolerated the inherent mess of art making on a grand scale.

The early elementary students, kindergarten through second grade, who created the amazing art shown here.

Jeanne Berlin whose technical and artistic skills have again produced a book that is visually beautiful while being user friendly.

Janet Lorch who again created a beautiful cover and lent her professional expertise to fine tune the final copy. I love looking at her design work as much as looking at a fine work of art.

Table of Contents

Introduction

It was never my intention to be an elementary art teacher. If I did have a plan for my life work it was to be a college ceramic instructor. While attending Cranbrook Academy of Art to earn an MFA in ceramics in order to reach that goal, I took on a part-time job teaching art at a Montessori pre-school.

The ease and enjoyment I felt teaching the four and five year olds at the Montessori school should have altered my career aspirations but they didn't. After Cranbrook I was unable to find a college position and instead worked in the museum studio program at the Flint Institute of Arts. Once again working with youth seemed a natural fit.

It took me twelve years at the FIA to have the courage to admit to myself I should be teaching elementary art. I took some college classes to get my long expired teaching certificate renewed and was hired in the Lamphere School District. The rest is history and one of the results was this book, Animals, Houses & People.

My position at Lamphere has been based on a program called the Art Enhancer. As an Art Enhancer I make connections to the classroom teacher's curriculum, enhancing the learning through art. For example, when the second graders were studying whales, I had them make a life-size inflatable whale they could all fit into.

Another part of my position has been 'release time'. Here the classroom teacher brings her students to the art room for a designated time, half an hour to an hour, giving the teacher release time for planning and preparation. For most of the students this is their first encounter with art.

In the pages of Animals, Houses & People I've tried to show how I interpreted my position at Lamphere with early elementary. I've always considered the art room a magical place, almost sacred. It is a place where students can explore ideas, materials and all the while their creative processes are being validated.

A kindergarten teacher told me her students ask every day, "Is today art day?" When my position changed and I would not be teaching release time for kindergarten the next year, the teacher replied, "Oh no! You are their favorite teacher." Forgive these self-congratulatory statements, but aside from making my chest swell with pride it is part of the reason I have felt compelled to write Animals, Houses & People – to share the awesome honor and responsibility early elementary art educators have.

I hope it doesn't take you twelve years, as it did me, to realize teaching early elementary is really where it's at. When you plant a flower seed, the most important part of its growth is in those early stages: preparing the soil, watering, sunlight, weeding. And so it is with teaching: those early years are crucial. I hope Animals, Houses & People will be a valuable asset; my gift to you.

What is Extreme?

When Hiller Elementary did a whole-school theme on the difference one person can make, Walt Disney was used as an example. Second graders made a cardboard walk-through Cinderella castle complete with cardboard characters.

Extreme is:

- Big
- Risk taking
- Transforming the classroom, the school, the community.
- Altering the environment.
- Embracing new technology
- Inviting others to participate: teachers, parents, community leaders.
- Being outrageous.
- Trusting in yourself, trusting in your students.
- Pushing the limit, walking on the edge
- Being bold

Where do Extreme ideas come from?

My father, (who was a creative thinker himself), used to ask where my ideas came from. He speculated I could snatch them out of the air, like a magician plucking coins from nowhere. While it is somewhat mysterious where creative ideas originate, I am constantly 'tending my garden' for the sprouting of creative, fertile ideas. Here are some of my many garden patches.

- State and National Conferences, learning the new, expanding horizons. Attending is imperative to keep abreast of what's new. Giving presentations is even better. By giving, you in return receive.
- Travel, broadening horizons. Breaking away from usual routines is stimulating. A simple weekend getaway or extended time in another country are beneficial. Seek out fellowships that provide free intensive travel with like minded teachers.
- Find time to be still.
- Read art magazines; *School Arts, Arts & Activities, Metropolis.*
- Go to student art shows, galleries, museums. Take notes, sketch, take pictures.
- Exercise.
- Make my own art. Always keeping time, space and energy for this. Nothing speaks, (actually radiates), more directly to my students than this commitment.

Extreme is a state of mind. What was once a courageous extreme experience can, over time become just another of your bag of incredible teaching tricks. For me it is usually the third time I do the extreme, (such as making an inflatable), that I feel comfortable with it and it becomes the usual instead of the extreme.

Don't be surprised if your students don't know they are venturing into the extreme. But the excitement and even the uncertainty you radiate will transfer to them. And this is good because their buy-in participation will be necessary to see the project through.
Your students will also see you in the process of creative thinking, problem solving. This is much different than teaching from a tried and true cookbook type lesson, (which we all do at times). This may be one of the greatest gifts you have to offer your students, the modeling of the creative thinking process.

Finally, Extreme Art is less for your students and more for yourself. It keeps you vibrant. Be the type of teacher who teaches twenty years. Not the teacher who taught one year twenty times.

Animals

Animals and young children seem to hold a special affinity for one another. When we turned a weedy courtyard into a goldfish pond/sculpture garden at school I introduced a rabbit into the area. Shadow, our black mini Rex was skittish about letting students pet her, except for the kindergartners. She would allow their small hands to stroke her soft fur; as if she seemed to sense their smallness and innocence.

Animals have provided inspiration for art making since the beginning of art making. Deep in the recesses of caves in France, horses, rendered in charcoal, adorn the stone walls drawn 40,000 years ago. Artists still interpret animals in their own time and style. Contemporary artist Deborah Butterfield's sculptural horses exude the same attraction/affection for horses as did those cave artists of another time and place.

Animals as subjects for lessons and innovative projects are limitless. In this section I've included lessons from the tiny to the huge and from individual to whole class projects. Pencils, paint, clay, collage and visquene plastic provide a variety of materials for students to shape their responses to the animal world.

From left to right, Jill Richardson, Sonny's owner, Carol Hinshaw and Jen Cumiskey, the principal, watch as a first grader offers apple slices to Sonny.

Bringing a Horse to School

Bringing a live animal to class to use as a visual creates excitement and motivation that a flat, two-dimensional picture never could. The animal's three-dimensionality, movements, sounds and even smells provide extreme stimulation for art making. The extra effort it takes in bringing the animal will also leave a positive and indelible impression on the students. Over my years of teaching I have brought a menagerie of animals into the classroom including piglets, a mouse, a rabbit, a turtle, a chicken, grasshoppers and even a llama. Asking a friend to bring her horse to school took a little more thought and planning: receiving permission from the school administration, rescheduling classes so all the students could see and pet Sonny and convincing the principal to ride bareback for a photo op. But the payback was more than worth it in the multitude of horse lessons that followed.

Pieces of masonite were used as drawing boards for students to sketch Sonny.

For the day I rented chaps, a vest and a cowboy hat from a costume shop.

Many of the drawings showed acute observational skills.

Along with Sonny, Jill brought old horse magazines which the students used for collages.

Painting with Tempera

Horse painting has a rich history. 40,000 years ago artists rendered horses on cave walls with charcoal. 16th century Persian miniature paintings depict hunting scenes with archers on horseback. And in the 20th century Franz Marc painted horses red, emphasizing the expressive nature of color.

Because Sonny was a chestnut brown I encouraged students to use brown for their horse painting. Some students found this limiting as can be seen in the blue hooves.

Young students are able to paint a horse following these step-by-step procedures: beginning with the largest parts and finishing with the smaller details. The fluid consistency of the tempera coupled with the brush strokes will capture the feeling of a running horse.

Materials:

- tempera paint
- brushes
- paint containers
- water containers
- white paper
- paper towels
- smocks
- copies of "drawing a horse", one per student

There are many great horse artworks which I showed during this unit. This poster shows a painting by W.R. Leigh that hangs in the Joslyn Art Museum, Omaha, Nebraska.

Procedures:

Display pictures of both real horses and the colorful horse paintings of Franz Marc. *Red Horses* is a good example because it shows three horses in different positions. Call attention to how Marc has used his imagination to change the color of the horses to red.

1. Paint the oval body.
2. Paint the neck and head.
3. Paint the legs and tail.
4. Add details: mane, ears, hooves, eye.

Investigating the nature of tempera, experimenting with color mixing and capturing the image of a horse on paper.

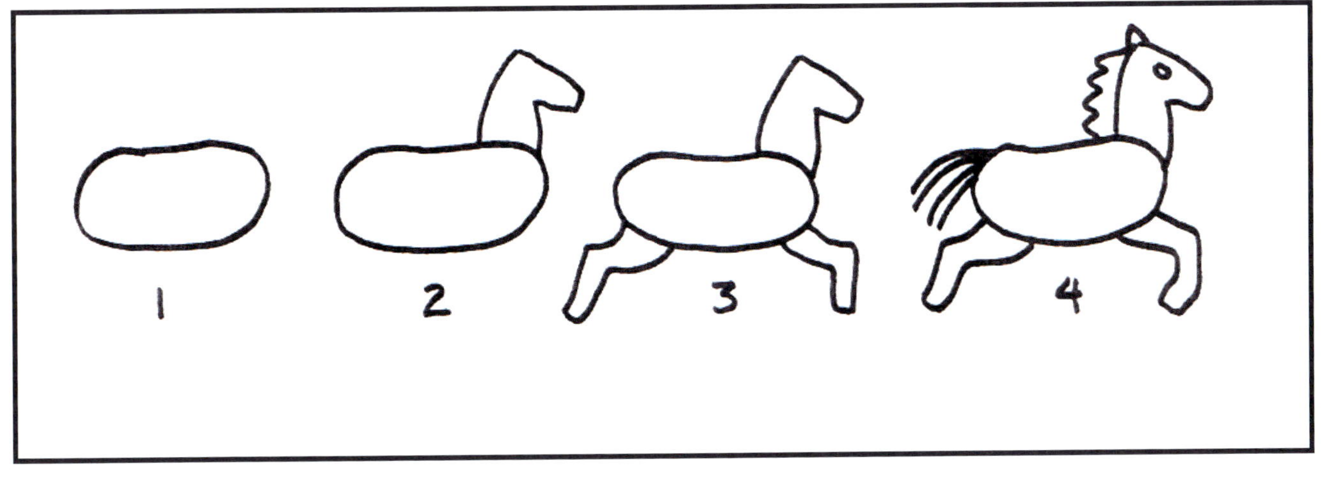

Clay Horses

The clay horses of the Tang Dynasty are more horse than horse. The Chinese artists have accentuated the horse's attributes making them more beautiful than a real horse could ever be. The ears are alert, nostrils flared and leg muscles tense as if waiting expectantly for a rider to mount.

This first grade horse appears alert and waiting for a rider.

Shaping a horse in clay follows the same procedures as with painting a horse, beginning with the largest and finishing with the smallest details. Constructing the horse on a clay slab, as are the Tang horses, will help it stand and lessen the chance of legs breaking off. While most students were satisfied with making a horse, some students added a saddle and a few even included a rider.

Materials:

- clay: either pottery or plasticine
- clay tools
- glazes or paints
- small cardboard pallets
- pictures of Chinese Tang Dynasty horses

Ceramic horses from the Tang Dynasty provided powerful visuals.

Procedures:

Prior to class I rolled a slab and cut clay bases, approximately 2" x 4". Students can also shape a base by flattening a piece of clay on the cardboard pallet.

1. Shape the body; somewhat of a stubby, short hot dog shape.
2. Shape a 'strong' neck. At the top of the neck bend the clay down and shape a head. By shaping the head from the neck rather than adding a head to the neck, it will be less likely to break off as the clay dries. Attach the neck to the body.
3. Roll and shape four legs. The legs should be fatter than real horse legs in order to support the clay body. Attach the legs to the body and also to the base.
4. Note: It is important all the pieces be well attached. If the clay is dry students can use a little water to aid adhesion.
5. Add a tail, small pointed ears and mane. Use a toothpick or sharpened pencil to etch in the hair in the tail and mane. Draw eyes.
6. Allow to dry. Bisque fire. Glaze and refire.

At a museum shop I bought inexpensive Tang reproductions for the students to use as visuals.

A simple, honest and charming kindergarten clay horse.

Carousel Horses

When I ask students how many had ridden on a carousel horse, nearly every hand goes up. So while many students had never seen a real live horse prior to Sonny coming to school; most have ridden a horse even if it was only made of wood.

Carousel horses are considered a form of American folk art. Thousands were carved by hand during the heyday of amusement parks and traveling fairs around the turn of the century. While it is still possible to ride an original carved wooden horse, many are now housed in museums and private collections.

The more decorative and colorful the better; at least on this horse.

Materials:

- horse pattern traced and cut on stiff paper or watercolor paper
- black permanent felt tip
- watercolors
- rhinestones or sequins
- wood bead
- bamboo skewer
- wood block
- craft glue

Increase 400%

Procedures:

I cut out a horse pattern for each student. The classroom teachers did not feel most of their students could effectively cut them out and the project had already been designated as a Christmas gift for their parents.

I also drilled a hole in a scrap piece of wood molding for each horse's base.

1. With permanent black felt tip draw a saddle, bridle, eyes, decorative ornamental harness, etc.
2. Paint with watercolors, (crayons or markers may be substituted).
3. When dry, glue on rhinestones or sequins.
4. Glue to bamboo skewer. Glue a wood ball or bead to the top of the skewer. Glue skewer into wood block.

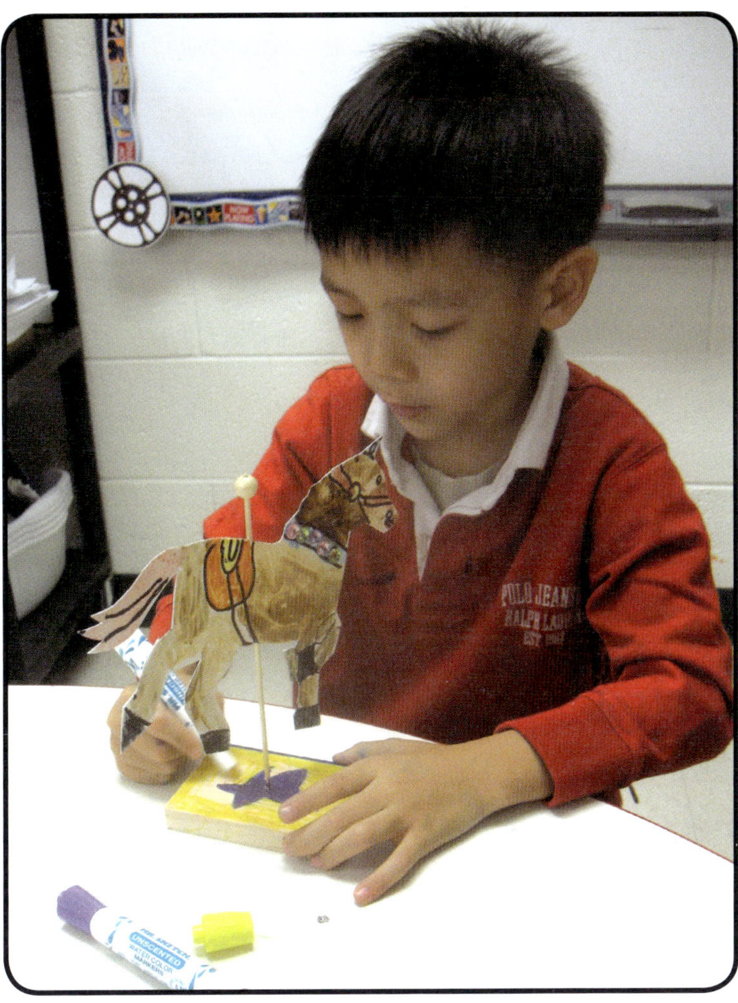

Although I had hoped to have students paint the bases, this student didn't wait and simply used markers.

My wife Carol and I toured the Carousel Museum in Sandusky, Ohio. It is hard not to smile when riding a painted pony!

Extreme Art

Sonny made from cardboard boxes, a discarded mop mane, a yarn tail and tempera paint.

A Life-Size Cardboard Sonny

Large cardboard boxes, free for the taking, can be cut, assembled and glued to make near life-size animals. Dinosaurs, giraffes, elephants, alligators and llamas have all been shaped or assembled with my help and painted by my elementary students. The large scale animals have made an impressive display in the school lobby.

Sonny received many coats of paint from eager students.

Deborah Butterfield is a contemporary American artist who makes life-size horses from found and selected sticks and branches. The finished horse is then cast in bronze. Instead of assembling our horse from sticks, we used found cardboard boxes.

Deborah Butterfield, American b 1949
Tarkio
Bronze, 2011
96x101x50 in.
Collection of the Flint Institute of Arts, Flint, Michigan
Gift of the Hurand Family and Museum, Purchase Fund 2011.131
Art © Deborah Butterfield/Licensed by VAGA, New York, NY

Penguins

Making small clay penguins allowed second grade students the opportunity to demonstrate what they were learning about penguins. This included the varieties of species of penguins and their habitats. They made the species that they found the most intriguing. This project was finished as a snow globe; making reference to the birds' frozen habitat.

An emperor and rock hopper penguin.

Materials:

- clay: pottery or plasticine
- glazes
- small jar, such as a baby food jar
- glitter
- aquarium glue

Procedures:

1. With a golf ball size piece of clay shape a penguin. Make a small clay base and attach the penguin. Add feet. Draw in wings.

2. Push a pencil up through the penguin facilitating the drying process.

3. Allow to dry, bisque fire, glaze and refire.

Note: Plasticine clay may be used in place of the pottery clay which makes firing unnecessary.

Students referred to a specific species when shaping and glazing their penguin.

Extreme Art

The finished penguin was displayed in the school library.

Penguins

Materials:

- chicken wire
- wire clippers
- staple gun
- 2' x 2' plywood base
- 2" x 2" x 3' wood support
- heavy duty aluminum foil
- masking tape
- wheat paste or wall paper paste
- newspapers
- tempera paint

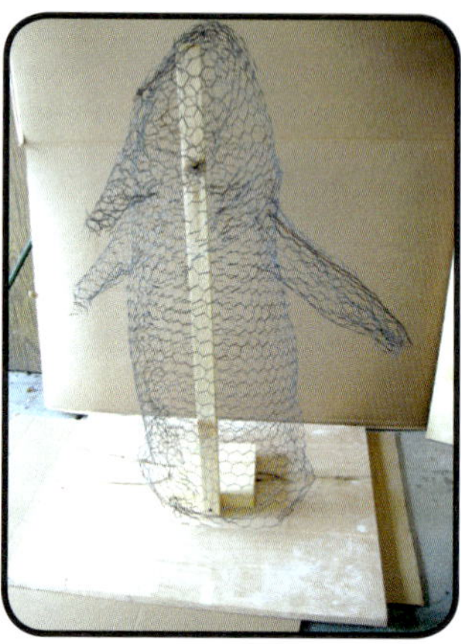

Chicken wire armature with wood support.

Procedures:

Note: The chicken wire armature should be made by an adult because it is difficult to cut and shape for young children. The wire is also sharp and cuts easily. Leather gloves suggested.

1. Cut 2" x 2" wood to approx. 3' length. Nail or screw to 2' square plywood base.
2. Cut and shape chicken wire to resemble penguin. Staple to wood base.
3. Cover with heavy duty aluminum foil and hold in place with masking tape.
4. Cover with three layers of papier mache.
5. After the papier mache is dry, 1 – 2 days, the penguin can be painted.

Call attention to your Extreme Art. This article was in our district newsletter, which is now done on-line. Call your local newspaper, invite school board members and the administration team.

DATELINE Lamphere

NEWSLETTER OF THE LAMPHERE SCHOOLS • MADISON HEIGHTS, MICHIGAN • JANUARY 20[illegible]

Penguin auction raises money for zoo

Lessenger Elementary School—Second and fourth graders in Mrs. Kathy Corriere's, Mrs. Pat Yakubison's, and Mrs. Chris Anderson's classrooms at Lessenger have completed a cross-age project on penguins. They did research in the library and the internet and brought in information from home. They wrote reports, prepared question and answer cards and did art work all pertaining to penguins.

With the help of Art Specialist Craig Hinshaw the students built a four-foot tall papier maché penguin. Not knowing who should get the penguin, the classes decided to hold a raffle. The students printed and sold raffle tickets to students, parents and anyone else who walked through Lessenger's doors. The raffle was held on LTV and fourth grader Amy George became the proud winner of a penguin.

Money raised in the raffle was donated to the Penguinarium at the Detroit Zoo. Students earned $180 and L.E.S.T. donated another $150 to bring the total donation to $330. Lessenger Principal Bernard Travnikar said, "Lessenger's second and fourth graders have made a difference. They have worked as a team and made a contribution to the community."

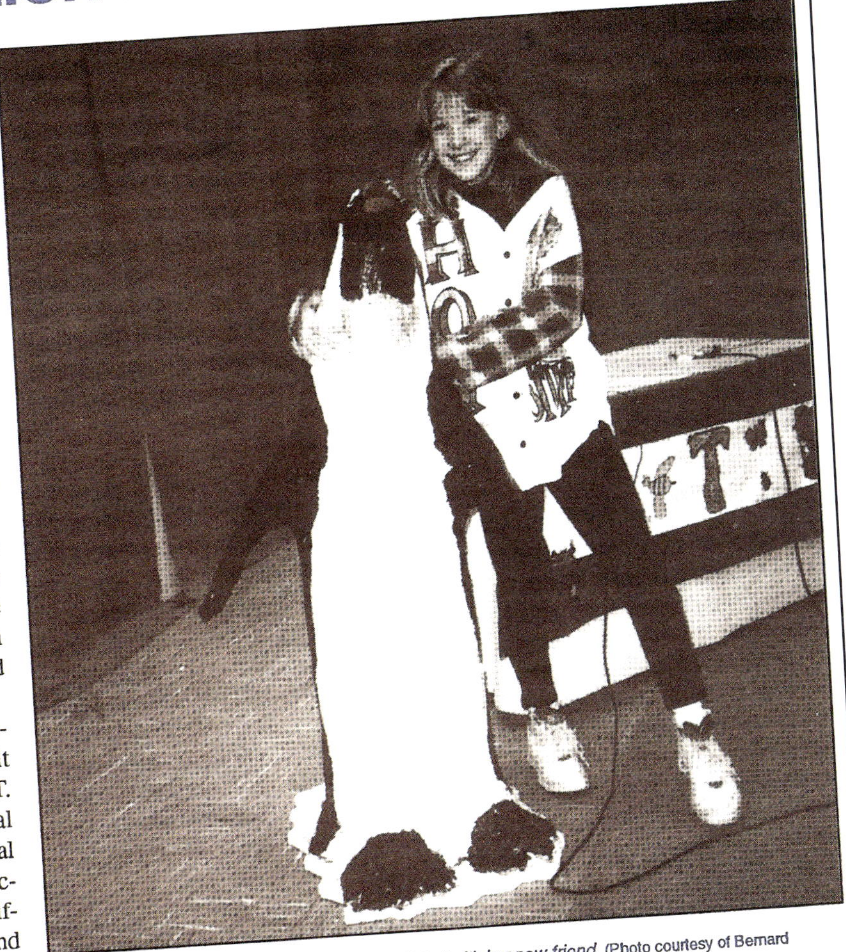

Penguin prize winner Amy George gets acquainted with her new friend. (Photo courtesy of Bernard Travnikar)

Butterfly Kites

Kites are toys. There is really no reason to fly a kite other than pure enjoyment. That's why I'm a kite flier and teach kite making.

A gentle wind turns the kite into a pet on a leash.

There are three parts to kite making with children:

1. Making or constructing the kite.
2. Decorating,
3. Flying.

There are correct procedures, measurements and proportions to kite making. But a piece of paper, a drinking straw, tape and string is all young children need to make a kite in their own way. In other words I show children the correct method but don't get hung up on variations children invent.

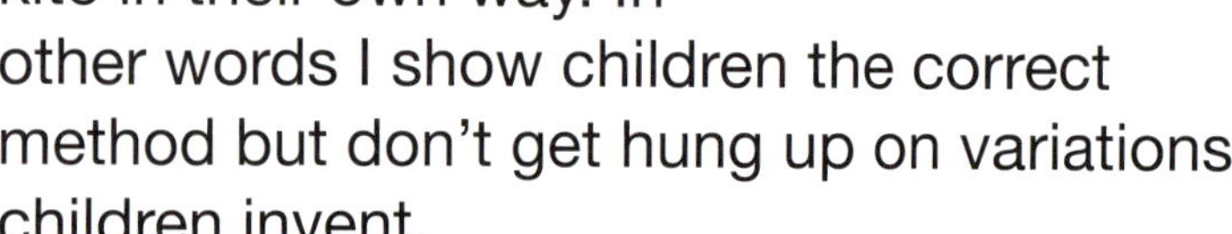

Materials:

- 8 ½ x 11" copy paper
- drinking straw
- tape
- string, about 3' long
- hole puncher
- paper reinforcement
- crayons
- permanent black marker
- crepe paper streamers
- stapler
- toilet paper tube, optional

Kite making is a good introduction to the concept of symmetry.

Procedures:

1. Fold the paper in half, book fold.
2. Along the folded crease, fold the kite's spine as shown.
3. Folds A and B should touch. Tape a drinking straw as shown.
4. Punch hole through spine. Add paper reinforcement.
5. Staple crepe paper streamers along the bottom. Tie on string.
6. Punch a hole in a toilet paper tube and tie the other end of the string to it.

Note: Many of the procedures children will need help with: folding, taping and tying string. A parent helper will make the lesson go smoother and allow time for flying.

A Chinese silk and bamboo kite.

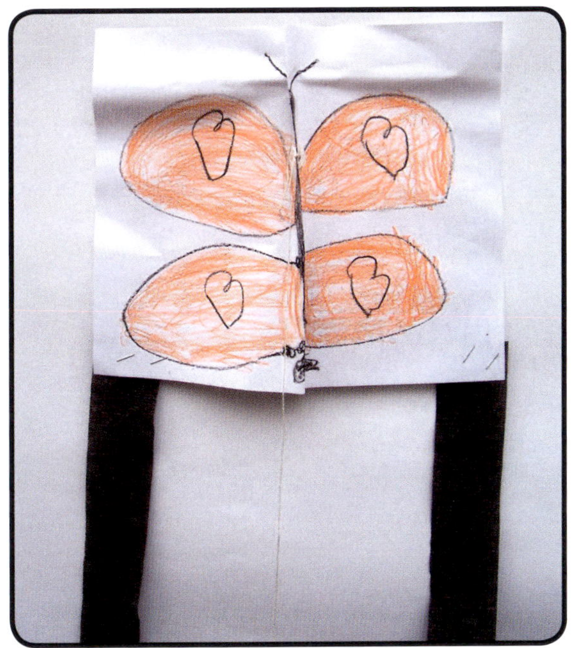

Kites allow students to touch the sky.

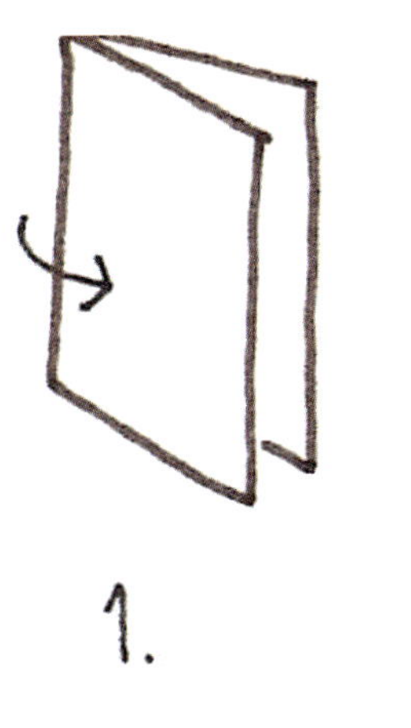

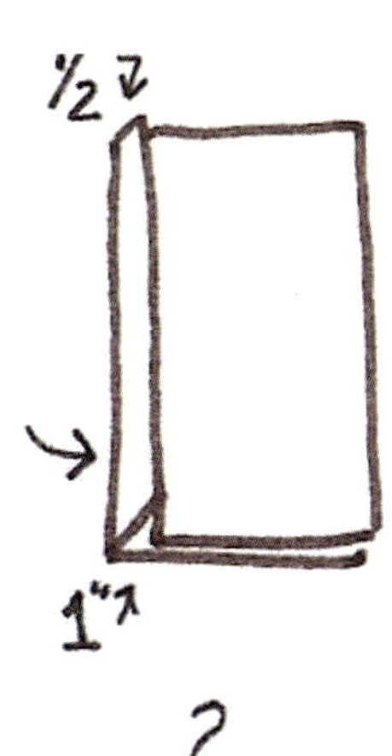

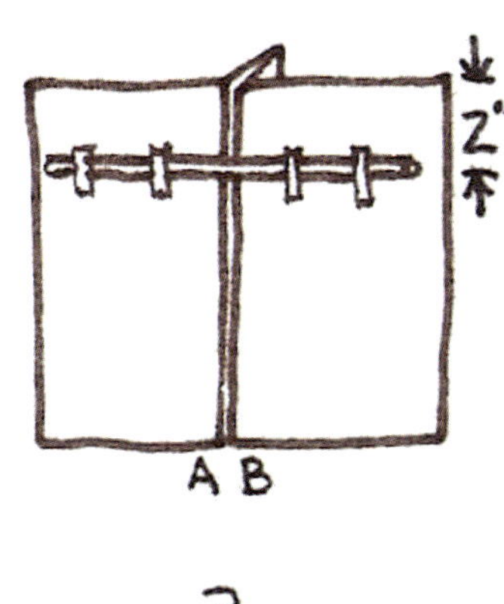

The enlarged butterfly was as large as the student who designed it.

B.U.G.S.

B.U.G.S. is the acronym for Being Unusually Good Students. It was thought up by the lunchroom moms in an effort to promote better discipline in the cafeteria. They asked if I could develop an art project that could be hung in the lunchroom as a visual reminder of the students' commitment to better behavior.

I began the project by having every student in the school draw and color a bug. I provided lots of visuals to stimulate their creative juices while getting a variety of insect types. One bug was selected from each grade level to be enlarged. The students' bug drawings were saved to use on t-shirts.

Large sheets of ½" foam core had been donated to the school by a design firm. I enlarged the selected bug drawings on butcher block paper and then cut them into body parts: abdomen, thorax, head, wings, antennae, etc. I traced these onto the foam core and cut them out using a scroll saw.

Student grade acrylic paint was mixed with pre-mixed wall paper paste and brushed onto the foam core. Students used large-tooth plastic combs, kitchen utensils and a variety of tools to inscribe lines and textures in the still-moist paste. New colors could be brushed on top and combed through, creating wonderful, textured paste-paper effects. While the paste was still wet the bug's body parts were reassembled sticking them together once the paste dried.

The final large five colorful bugs now hang in the cafeteria. Is the discipline better? I don't know. But I do know the lunchroom is a more attractive place to eat with the large colorful bugs decorating the stark white walls.

Materials:

- acrylic paint
- pre-mixed wallpaper paste
- brushes
- sheets of foam core (tempered Masonite could be used, although it is more difficult to cut and heavier to hang)
- combs, various kitchen utensils.

A large colorful beetle.

The original drawing used for the large foam core butterfly.

Paste paper technique creates a colorful textured surface.

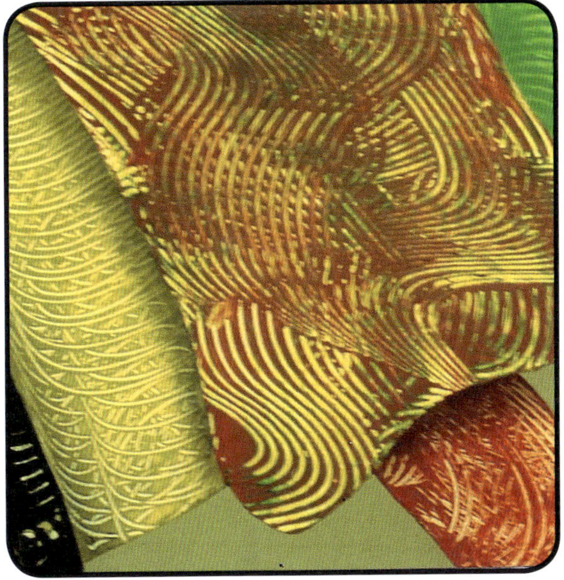
Detail of the textures and colors created by the paste-paper techniques.

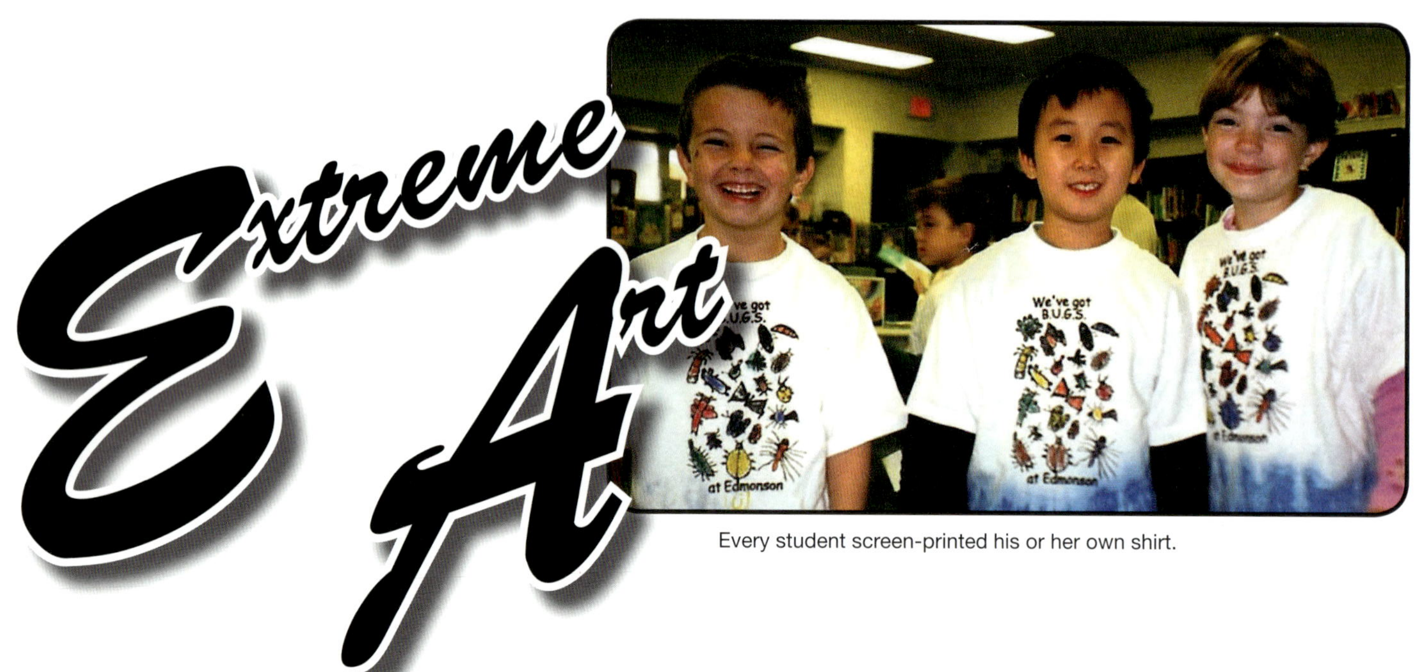

Every student screen-printed his or her own shirt.

B.U.G.S. T-Shirts

The bug drawings were used to create a different silkscreen for each classroom. The 20 to 25 drawings, one from each student in the class, were glued to a piece of 8 ½" x 11" paper with the words "We've Got B.U.G.S. at Edmonson." The stencils were created using a commercially available thermal screen-printing process.

The P.T.O. purchased a white T-shirt for every one of the 240 students and staff members. I moved from classroom to classroom, carrying the T-shirt press and black textile ink, and allowed the students to print their own shirt.

The following week the students used fabric markers (one set purchased for each classroom) and colored their bug T-shirts. Moms ironed every shirt permanently heat-setting both the black ink and the fabric marker.

Edmonson's colors are blue and white, so we tie-dyed the bottom part of the shirts next. Students accordion-folded the lower part of the shirt and used four to six rubber bands to "tie" it off in sections. Fifth graders helped the first grade students with the folding and rubber bands.

Relying on the help of moms again, the lower half of the tied shirts were immersed in large tubs of blue dye simmering on hot plates, for about 20 minutes. Then the excess blue dye was rinsed from the shirts and they were carried to the playground to dry in the sun. Amazingly, we dyed all the shirts in one day.

Materials:

- thermal screens and T-shirt press (sold commercially through most art supply distributors)
- black textile screen ink
- fabric markers
- fabric dye
- rubber bands
- hot plate
- large tubs

Students enjoyed wearing their screen-printed, colored and dyed shirts.

I use this small, light-weight t-shirt printing frame which is available commercially.

With over 300 shirts to tie-dye I enlisted the help of school moms

Origami Fish

The folded paper crane is the most well known origami. Although it is too difficult for young children to attempt, I demonstrate the folding as an introduction. I also tell them the story of the Japanese girl, Sadako, and how she attempted to fold 1,000 cranes while she was in the hospital.

Origami fish colored with markers.

This simple fish or shark is a good introduction to paper folding. I encourage students to check out origami books from our school library if they have enjoyed the lesson. And you never know, for some, this may become the start of a life- long hobby.

PS - Classroom teachers love the lesson because it makes a colorful bulletin board display.

Origami shark.

Stick glue effectively holds the folds in place.

Materials:

- 9" white paper square
- scissors
- glue or tape
- markers or crayons

Procedures:

The same fold is used for both the fish and the shark. Before class I cut 9"x 12" white paper into 9" squares and then cut the extra piece into 3" squares for 'baby' fish and sharks.

1. Fold into a triangle.
2. Fold again into a triangle.
3. Open.
4. Fold each corner to the center.
5. Open and cut the two creases where indicated.
6. Glue or tape creating a fish or shark and decorate.

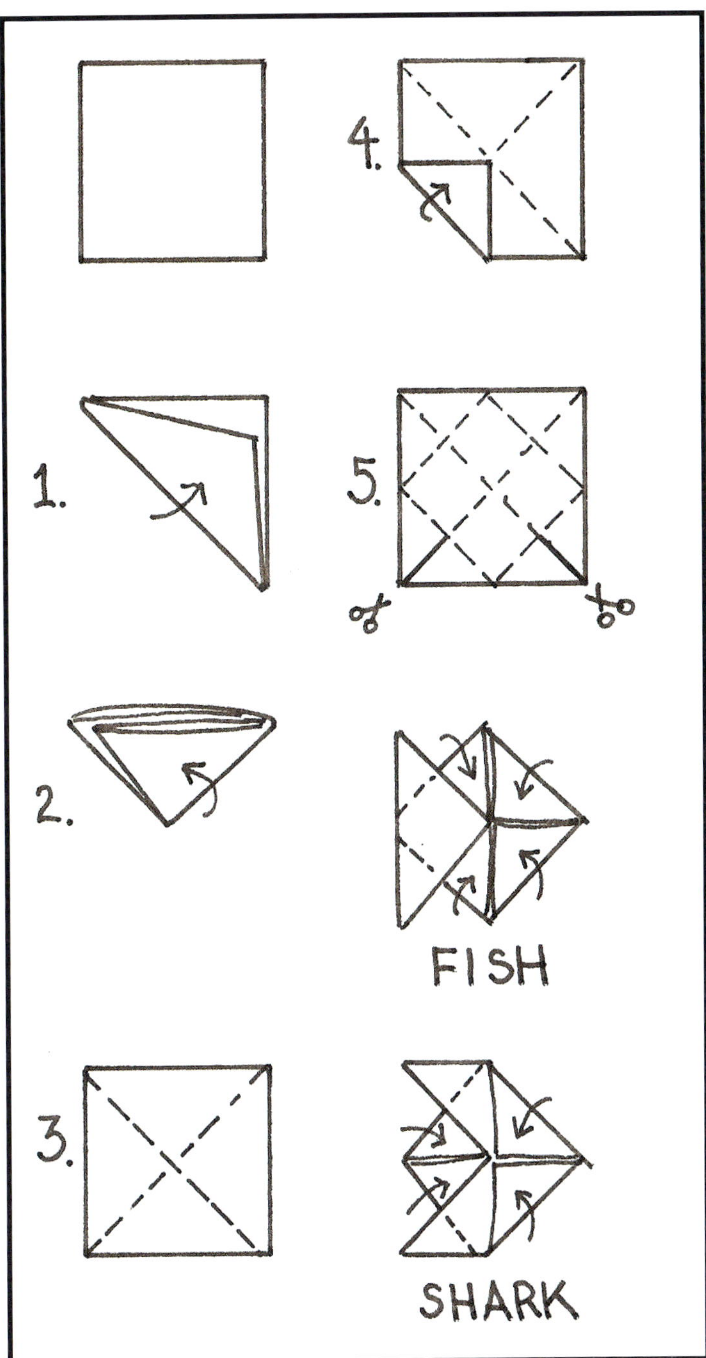

Suggested reading:
Sadako and the Thousand Paper Cranes
by Eleanor Coerr.

Much excitement and pride inside the belly of the whale.

A Life Size Whale of a Fish

A giant fish swallowed Jonah, Gepetto was swallowed by a whale as he searched for Pinocchio and now a whale has swallowed fifty second grade students! There are not many whales in Michigan so we made our own using visquene plastic, clear packing tape and a box fan to inflate the leviathan.

Although the finished inflated whale was huge, the time to make it took only the morning; each second grade working for about one hour cutting and taping. In the afternoon the classes spent time in the whale. I moved a VCR inside and we watched Burt Dow, Deep-Water Man by Robert McCloskey. I even taught an art lesson inside the whale: how to fold an origami whale. Later in the day other classes were invited to admire our whale and venture inside.

Materials:

- clear 4 mil visquene. This is sold in rolls at building supply stores.
- 2” clear packing tape, about 6 - 8 rolls.
- permanent markers
- box fan.

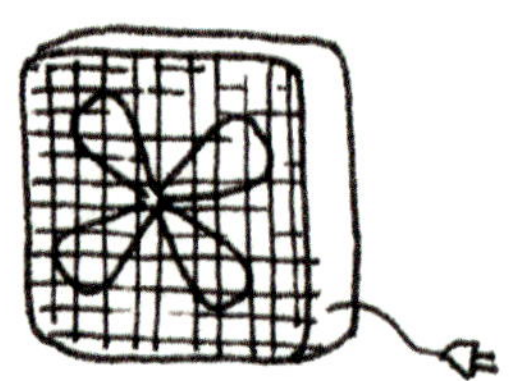

Procedures:

1. Unroll and unfold visquene on the floor. Refold it in half.

2. Draw outline of whale on top piece with a permanent marker. Cut through both pieces at once.

3. Place students in groups of two or three. One student unrolls and cuts and wraps the tape around the seam connecting the top and bottom pieces. All the seams should be taped except the end where the tail will be attached.

4. Double visquene, draw, cut and tape the tail and flippers. Connect them to the whale, making sure there is an opening between them allowing air to channel through. Make and attach a dorsal fin to the top.

5. Along the side cut an "x" large enough to place the box fan in. Inflate.

6. When the whale is nearly inflated, cut a three foot vertical slit along the side to create the door and allow some air to escape. Otherwise the over-inflated whale will begin tearing off the tape.

7. Take off shoes and go inside – too cool!

8. Students may work inside and outside patching air leaks.

Students worked in pairs cutting tape then taping the seams.

The whale was large enough to allow students to stand inside. The tail and flippers were made from thinner garbage bag plastic sold on rolls.

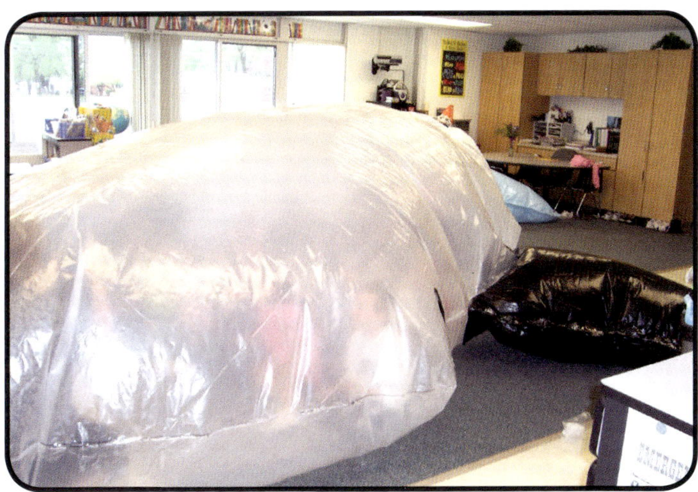

The whale filled the classroom then swallowed the class.

Rod Puppets-Toilet Paper Tubes

When teaching a puppet lesson, I let my puppet example introduce the lesson. Speaking in his puppet voice, the puppet gives instructions and even carries on a conversation with me. Aside from capturing the students' attention, it begins teaching how to operate the puppet and even present a puppet show.

A boy cat puppet in blue jeans.

Puppets, like kites, are a magical toy which completely engrosses young students. They treat their puppet like an imaginary friend, like many students have at this young age, looking at and talking with their puppet intently.

At the end of class I show how to operate the puppet and have the students experiment with various puppet voices.

Materials:

- toilet paper tubes
- felt
- bamboo skewers
- white glue
- craft glue
- felt tips
- construction paper
- tissue paper
- wiggle eyes

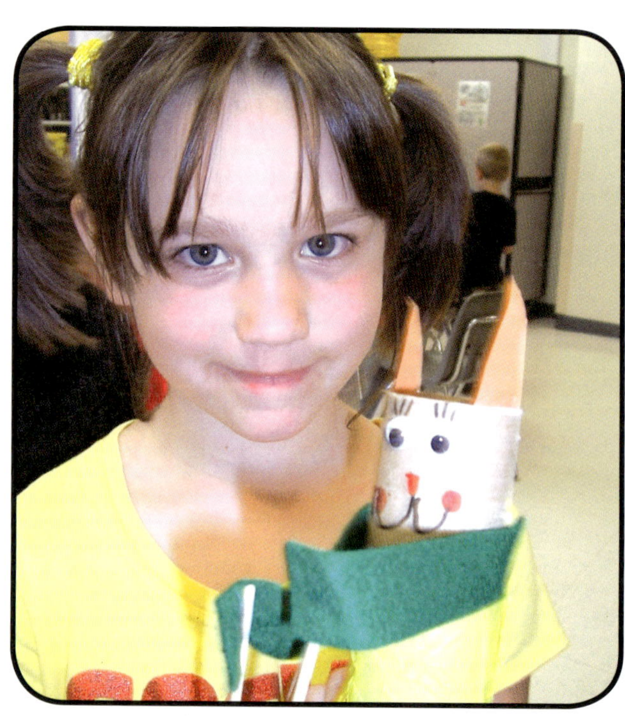

A girl bunny puppet with a yellow dress.

Procedures:

The day before class cut felt into 1" x 6" strips. With heavy scissors or tin snips cut the sharp ends off the bamboo skewers, (2 per puppet). Glue the two felt strips half way down on the toilet paper tube creating arms. Glue the skewers to the other end of the felt strips. Allow to dry.

1. Suggest students make a cat, rabbit or dog puppet. Cutting and gluing on colorful construction paper ears begins to transform the toilet paper tube into a puppet.

2. For a boy puppet, make pants by wrapping and gluing a piece of 6" x 3" construction paper below the arms. Cut triangle slits defining the legs. For a girl puppet, glue a 3" x 8" piece of tissue paper below the arms to create a dress.

3. Glue on wiggle eyes.

4. Finish with markers.

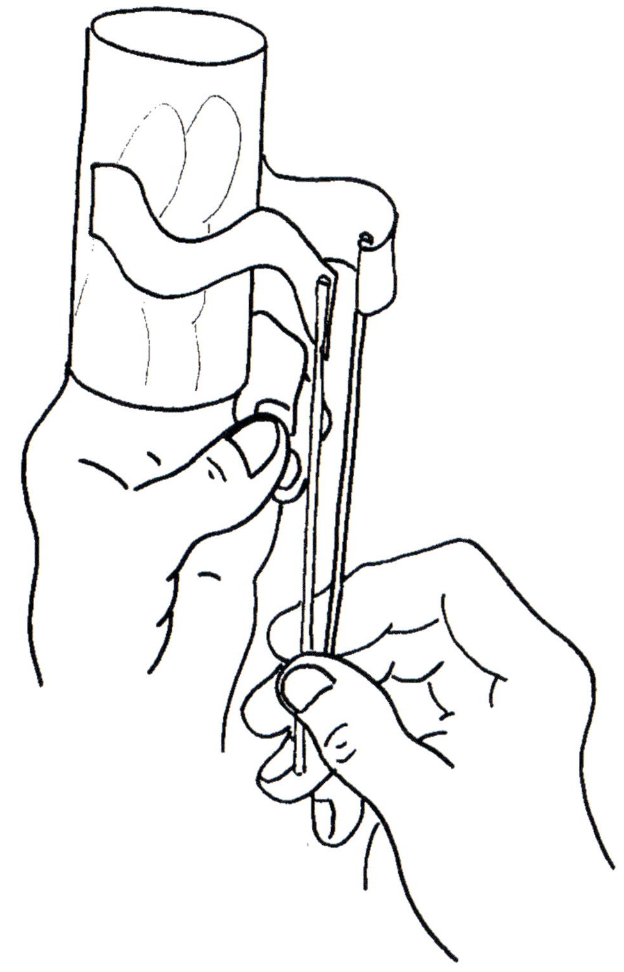

Operating the puppet.

The index finger and middle finger of one hand go inside the tube holding it upright. The other hand holds the ends of the skewers, operating the arms. Practice scratching the head as if thinking, hiding the eyes as if embarrassed, rubbing the tummy after a good meal. Give your puppet a 'puppet' voice; deep and low or perhaps squeaky and high pitched.

Extreme Art

Math Cat at the Heidelberg Project.

Math Cat - A Giant Rod Puppet

Jim Henson expanded the way we think of puppets, even changing the name of his Sesame Street community from puppets to Muppets, (marionette + puppet). But giant puppets have been around long before Bert and Ernie appeared on TV. Today giant puppets are often seen in parades.

The school's mascot is the wildcat and the school's colors are red and white; hence we made a red cat head. Math Cat's first performance was at the school board meeting where students introduced our new math curriculum. The giant puppet is operated by three students, one inside holding up the head and two operating the hands.

Math Cat took the coordinated effort and practice of three students to operate.

Materials:

- clay
- wall paper paste or wheat paste
- newspapers
- tempera paint
- fabric
- cardboard or foam core (for hands)
- bamboo
- black nylon screen wire
- wood pole
- saran wrap

Giant puppets at a street parade in Oaxaca, Mexico.

Procedures:

1. Math Cat's papier mache head was first made from two slabs of clay. Clay ears, whiskers, nose and eyes were added. I did this.

2. The form was covered with plastic wrap. This would allow easy release of the papier mache from the clay once it had dried.

3. Students covered the head with 3 – 5 layers of strips of newspaper, (approx. 2" x 8"), saturated in wheat paste.

4. A razor knife was used to cut along the sides of the head and peeled it off of the clay form. Glue and more strips of the papier mache were used to reconnect the head. The clay head was reclaimed for other art projects.

5. Tempera paint was used to paint the head.

6. The school secretary made Math Cat's fabric body. A rectangle of black nylon screen was sewn in the chest area, allowing the student inside holding up the head with a wood pole to see out. The hands were cut from ¼" foam core and connected to the fabric sleeves with Velcro.

Robins

One of the first signs of spring is the return of the robins. Here in Michigan they always seem to arrive too soon, often snow still covers the ground and hides the worms they look for to eat. This simple step-by-step method to draw a robin produces cute, colorful art by which all students can be successful, and perfect for a spring bulletin board.

Robin and tulips, one of the first signs of spring.

Charley Harper was an Ohio artist/illustrator who drew wonderfully stylized birds. He did not draw in a realistic manner, he simplified the bird to its basic geometric shapes and employed vivid colors. Harper, in jest said, “I don’t count the feathers, I just count the wings”.

Materials:

- white paper
- colored felt tips
- white paper reinforcements

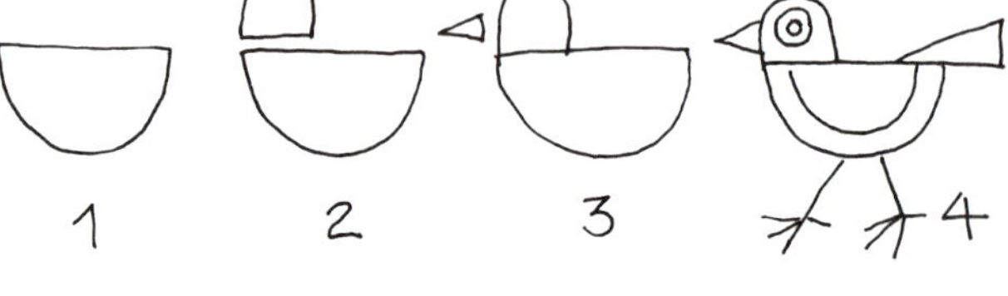

Procedures:

1. Draw a half-circle for the robin’s body.
2. Draw a smaller half-circle for the head.
3. Add a beak, tail and legs.
4. Draw the wing. A flying robin is made by drawing the wing ‘up’.
5. Color the head solid black. Place paper reinforcement on the head, creating the robin’s distinctive white rimmed eye.
6. Finish coloring the robin with a red breast.
7. Draw tulips, another sign of spring and a fat worm in the grass.

Charley Harper, Baltimore Orioles

While I imagined robins, the students were more creative in their painting.

Papier Mache Birds

A row of black birds sitting on an overhead line. They seem to be chattering to one another, moving close as if to listen, then moving apart. It is this daily image outside of the school which inspired the following lesson.

Lined up in the library, the colorful birds seemed to be chattering with each other.

I imagined a row of kindergarten made birds, lined up in a long row on the bookshelves in the school library. I imagined all the birds painted the same; perhaps as robins. All went according to my plans until I got out the paint, of which the students had more imagination than I.

Materials:

- wood base with bamboo skewer
- newspapers
- masking tape
- papier mache
- tempera paint
- brushes
- awl

Continued on next page

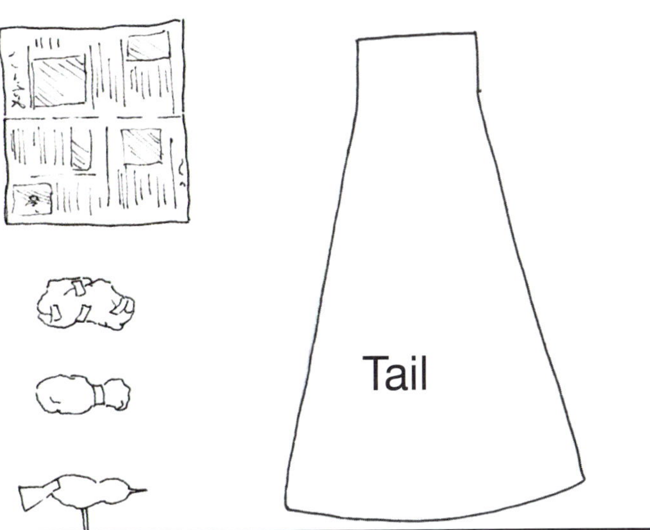

Extreme Art - Papier mache Birds continued

Procedures:

I made the wood bases by cutting a 4 inch square from scrap lumber, drilling a hole in the center and gluing a bamboo skewer in. I clipped off the skewer points and saved them for the birds' beaks. I also cut cardboard tails for each bird.

Class #1

1. Each bird is made from one double piece of newspaper. Crumple the newspaper into an oval shape. Secure with masking tape.
2. Squeeze the newspaper where the neck would be and secure with a piece of masking tape; like adding a collar. This defines the head and body.
3. Tape on the cardboard tail.
4. Tape on the pointed end of the skewer for the beak. A beak may also be shaped by pinching the newspaper and securing with tape.
5. With an awl, I punched a hole in the 'belly' of each bird and inserted it onto the skewer.
6. Secure the bird with tape: almost 'mummy like'.

Class #2

1. Tear newspaper into strips, approximately 1" x 4".
2. Mix wheat paste or wall paper paste and water.
3. Dip newspaper strips, one at a time, into the wheat paste and cover the bird with two layers.

Class #3

1. When dry, paint the bird with tempera paint.

After the bird is shaped in newspaper, it is covered with tape.

The birds are covered with two layers of papier mache and allowed to dry one week.

Painting a three-dimensional object was a new experience for most students.

Foam Masks

When a child makes and wears a mask, (particularly an animal mask), he is transformed, hiding behind this 'face shield'. Any inhibitions there might have been dissipate. The child, as well as a whole class, become wild things as they act out the animal their mask depicts.

The intent of this lesson was twofold: to make a mask but also to expand the students' ideas of what can constitute art materials beyond paper, crayons, etc. The students decided on an animal whose characteristics they would like to emulate: the ferocity of a lion, the silly antics of a monkey or perhaps the lightning speed of a jaguar. These are half masks, covering only their eyes and noses.

Pointed ears and whiskers allowed the student to become a cat. She holds a shadow puppet, see page 56.

Materials:

- carpet padding foam, (stiff paper will also suffice)
- craft glue
- felt tip markers
- scissors
- 1/4" braided elastic
- mirrors

Making masks from carpet foam expands the students' knowledge of what can constitute art materials.

Wood jaguar mask from Oaxaca, Mexico.

Procedures:

Prior to class, I cut the foam into approximately 12" x 6" rectangles and cut two eye holes in each.

1. Decide on an animal for the mask. Pictures of animals and animal masks will help stimulate ideas.
2. The eyes are an important part of the mask. Call attention to them with markers, outlining them or drawing eye lashes.
3. Cut and glue ears, nose and other decorative additions.
4. Note: Use ample glue and just lay the cut foam over the glue. Do not push the foam together or the glue will go into the foam, rather than connect the pieces.
5. Finish with colored markers.

Allow the masks to dry flat. Before the next class, I punched two holes in the sides of the mask and tied in the elastic band.

The masks turned the students into Hiller Wildcats for a kindergarten graduation performance.

Plaster Gauze Masks

It is not unusual for young children to discover mask making as they explore cutting paper with a pair of scissors. One or two holes cut in a piece of paper becomes something to look through and evolves into a mask. There is something inherently powerful, magical, in concealing one's face behind a mask while observing the reaction produced in others.

Plaster gauze mask making is usually taught to older grades but when a kindergarten teacher saw fifth graders wearing the animal masks they had made she convinced me to also make them with her students. I enlisted the fifth graders to help in applying the gauze to the kindergartners' faces. The teacher used the masks in a performance her students gave to the parents at kindergarten graduation.

Materials:

- plaster gauze, (an open weave fabric impregnated with plaster, sold through craft stores).
- petroleum jelly
- smocks
- plastic containers for water
- water
- quality scissors
- newspapers
- 1/4" braided elastic
- towels
- mirrors
- tempera paint

A student looks through one of my many masks I bring to class collected from my travels. This wood mask is from Mexico.

Procedures:

Class One:
Before class cut the plaster gauze into 3" x 1" strips. Each mask uses about forty strips.

Note: I only make half-masks which are light enough when finished to be worn without falling off.

1. With finger tips, smooth petroleum jelly over the face where the gauze will be applied: eye brows, nose, cheeks and upper lip. **Neither the eyes nor nostrils will be covered with gauze.**
2. Have students sit in chairs so they can lean their heads back, looking upward. Lay a smock or paint shirt over the student's neck and shirt/blouse. Although the project can be messy, plaster washes out of clothes and does not stain.
3. Dip one strip of gauze in warm water at a time, squeeze out excess by sliding the gauze between the index and middle fingers and cover the upper face with three layers.
4. For the kindergartners we had them lie on the carpet so their mask wouldn't slip off, (at this age their noses are so small the gauze would easily slide off).
5. The gauze dries enough to remove in 15 – 20 minutes. Set aside to dry on a piece of paper with the student's name on it.
6. Gently wash off petroleum jelly and bits of plaster from the students' faces.

Class Two:
1. Paint with tempera paint. Poster board ears may be added with hot glue. Glitter, feathers, pipe cleaners may also be used.

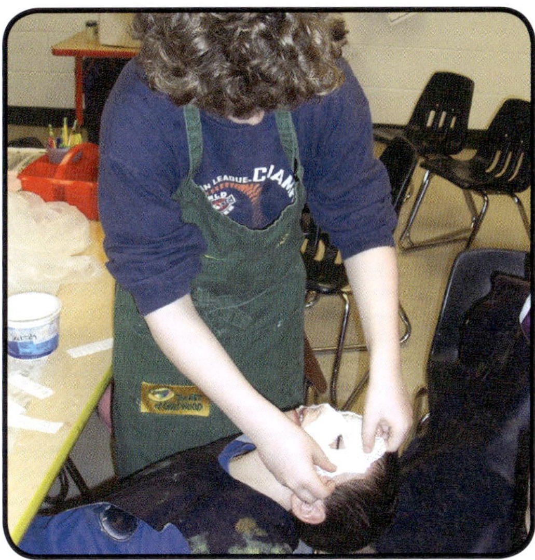

Fifth graders applied the moist gauze to the students' faces.

Kindergartners lay on their backs looking at themselves in mirrors waiting for the plaster to dry.

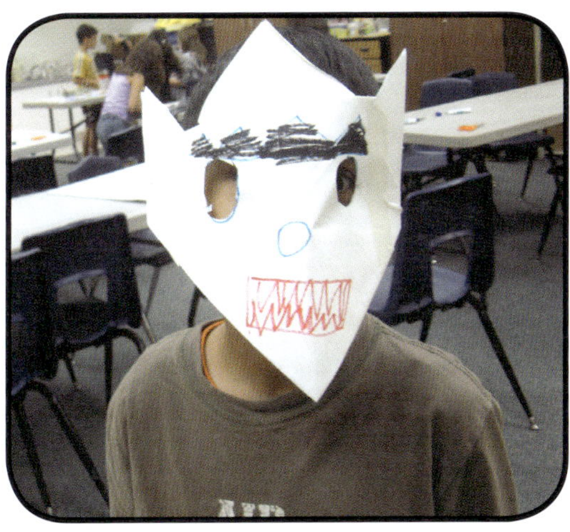

Mask making is something many students discover on their own.

Catching Lightning Bugs

Small pulsating dots of light illuminate Michigan nights. Lightning bugs are one of nature's incredible wonders. These little friendly insects that, neither bite nor sting, beckon to be caught by children.
When placed in a glass jar, the captured fireflies create a natural lantern.

Captured lightning bugs create a natural lantern.

Materials:

- 3" x 5" white paper
- 4 ½" x 6" construction paper in a variety of skin tones
- hole puncher
- pencils or black fine tip markers
- glue
- yellow fluorescent paint or fluorescent markers or yellow highlighter
- cotton swabs
- cups for paint

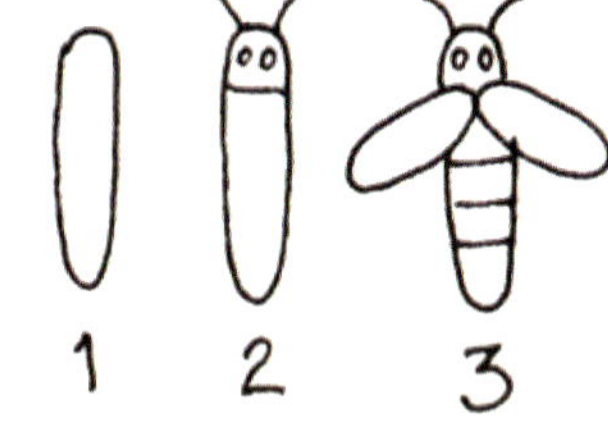

Procedures:

1. Show a glass jar and the 3" x 5" paper. Make the connection that the flat, rectangular piece of paper will represent the jar. Draw a line about ½-inch down from the top representing a lid. Punch holes in the lid providing air for the lightning bugs.

2. Draw flying lightning bugs in the jar.

3. With a cotton swab dot the lightning bug's abdomen with fluorescent paint, or use a fluorescent marker.

4. Trace and cut out a hand on the construction paper. Glue to the jar, wrapping fingers around as if holding the jar.

Suggested book: The Very Lonely Firefly by Eric Carle.

Easel brushes blend and soften the colors.

Sidewalk Art

In Mary Poppins, Bert, the sidewalk artist drew pictures that both he and Mary magically entered. Like Bert, artists today render amazing sidewalk art in hopes of receiving tips from admiring pedestrians. Through your instruction, the use of sidewalk chalk can become almost magical; far more than for hopscotch.

With many legs, wicked pinchers and black stripes, this insect is larger than the student.

Inside the classroom the students made a bug sketch on a small square of paper. Outside they helped sweep the sidewalk clean, then enlarged their sketch onto a square section of the cement. Easel brushes were used to blend and soften the colors.

Materials:

- sidewalk chalk, (For inexpensive chalk, Google railroad chalk which can be purchased in boxes of 144. The color is not as intense as the more expensive sidewalk chalk though.)
- stiff 1" easel brushes
- brooms, (allow students to help clean the sidewalk before drawing)
- step ladder, provides a better vantage to photograph
- buckets of water, sponges and towel, (the project can be messy)

Although faded from rain and foot traffic this mechanical butterfly still exhibits the layering of colors and extreme size - Cairns, Australia.

Tunnel Books

Robins fly past white clouds in a blue sky. Red tulips burst through green grass. A brilliant yellow sun shines over the spring landscape all told through this simplified tunnel book.

A tunnel book is a toy book you are drawn to look into, like those candy sugar Easter eggs with a small opening to view a miniature scene within. The 3-D quality makes the book sculptural in nature. The accordion folded sides allow the expanded book to be displayed either standing on a table or stapled to a bulletin board.

Kindergarten tunnel book announcing the arrival of spring.

Materials:

- 2 pieces 9" x 9" any color construction paper
- 1 piece 6" x 9" blue construction paper
- 1 piece 4" x 6" green construction paper
- 1 piece 2" x 6" green construction paper
- white paper
- crayons
- scissors
- glue

Top view showing construction.

Procedures:

For younger students I pre-fold the two accordion folded sides. Note: First I have students construct the book. Second they draw, color, cut out and glue in the robin, tulips, sun and clouds.

1. Glue the blue construction paper sky onto the back folds.
2. Cut an irregular 'grass-like' line along the 6" side of the green construction paper. Glue it onto the inside folds.
3. Cut an irregular 'grass-like' line along the 4" side of the green construction paper. Glue it to the front of the folded sides.
4. Draw, color, and cut a robin, tulips, sun, clouds, etc. and glue them into the assembled book.

Student viewing one of my peep-hole tunnel books.

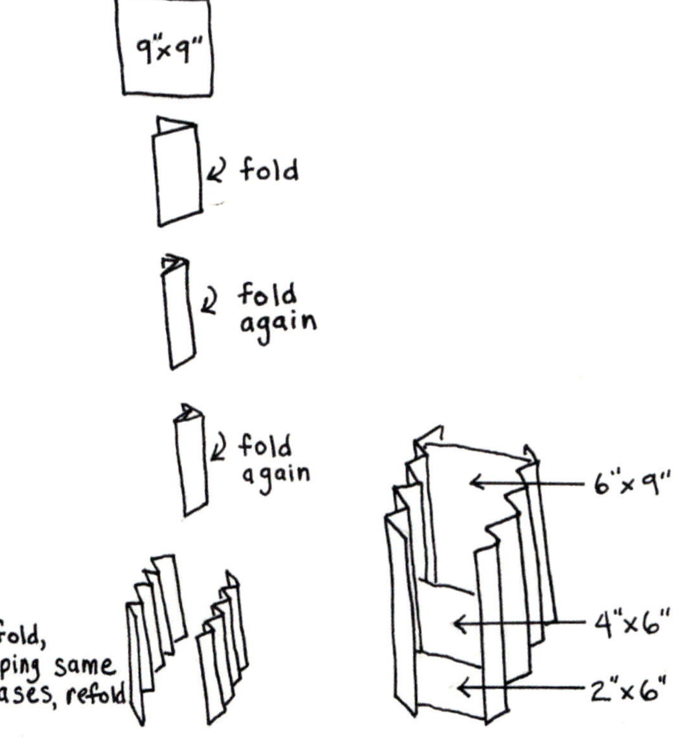

Completed first grade walk-through tunnel book.

A Walk Through Tunnel Book

While it might be unrealistic for a class of Michigan first graders to take a field trip to the ocean it didn't stop them from creating their own undersea environment. Larger than life-size clown fish, jellyfish and even killer whales inhabited the refrigerator cardboard and tempera paint walk-through tunnel book. The 'book' was displayed in the school library for the whole school to enjoy. The school was studying the oceans as a school-wide theme.

Large sheets of cardboard are perhaps the most expedient way to turn a school into an extreme environment. When our schools were studying Alaska, students made life-size polar, black and brown bears to show their size differences, (polar bears are the biggest). They also made a full team of husky dogs pulling a musher on a dog sled, all using scrap cardboard and tempera paint. A cardboard triangle glued to the back allows the cardboard cutouts to easily stand.

Materials:

- large sheets of cardboard: ask an appliance store to save some refrigerator boxes or purchase sheets from a box maker
- white sheets of cardboard
- tempera paint
- white glue
- utility knife

Procedures:

Note: A utility knife is used to cut the cardboard and should only be used by an adult!

1. I laid two open refrigerator boxes with the top and bottom pieces cut off on the floor with the printed side down. Students painted the cardboard with gradients of blue and white, lighter at the top. Newspapers were placed under the edges so the whole pieces were painted.

2. With a utility knife I scored the dried cardboard about every 2-feet, alternating the front and back. This allowed the cardboard to be accordion folded and stand self-supporting.

3. On pieces of white cardboard the students drew then painted an ocean animal. Once dry I cut them out with a utility knife and glued them onto the accordion folded sides.

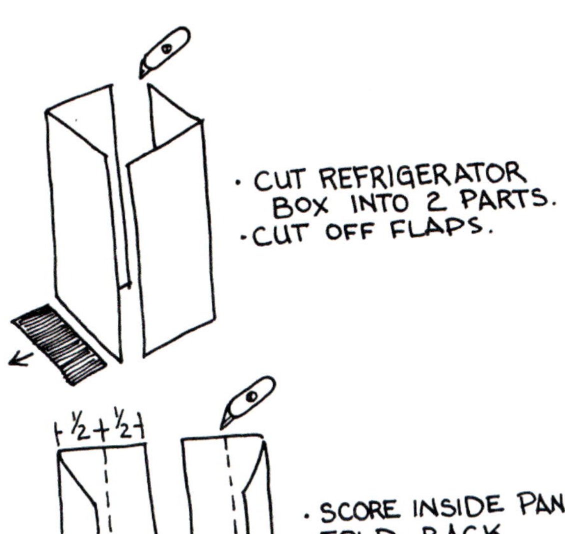

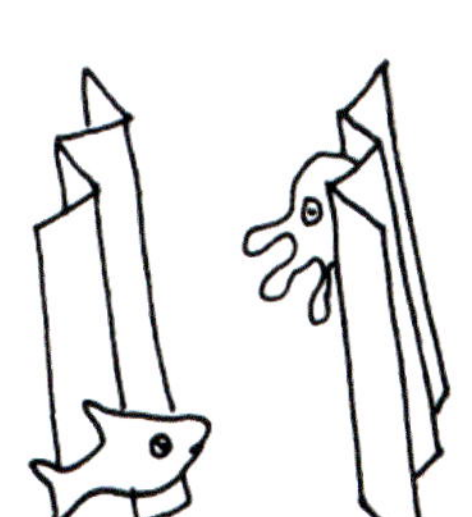

After students drew their images on cardboard I cut them out for them to paint.

Giant black ants crawling the walls and ceiling of Edmonson.

Catch the Reading Bug

When our school district's reading teachers adopted the slogan, *Catch the Reading Bug!,* we infested the school with ants; giant black ants. They crawled along the walls and ceiling of the main hallway.

The giant ants were made by covering inflated wiggle type balloons with papier mache. After the papier mache had dried and hardened, they were painted black and finished with black pipe cleaner legs and antennae. Velcro was used to hold the light-weight insects to the cinder block walls and metal supports of the drop ceiling.

Materials:

- wiggle type balloons
- wheat paste or wall paper paste
- newspapers
- plastic containers
- black tempera paint
- smocks
- black pipe cleaners
- hot glue
- Velcro

Procedures:

1. Inflate balloons.
2. Mix wheat paste or wallpaper paste and water. Tear newspaper into approximately 3" x 1" strips.
3. Dip one piece of newspaper in the wheat paste mixture at a time. Wipe off excess and lay over balloon. Cover entire balloon with three layers.
4. Allow to dry; about two days.
5. Paint with black tempera.
6. Adults attach legs and antennae with hot glue.

An ant held in place with Velcro on a metal ceiling support.

Kindergartners applied three coats of newspaper strips dipped in the wheat paste.

Groundhog Day

On Groundhog Day, February 2, the ground hog awakes from a winter's slumber and emerges from his hole. If the sun is out, as opposed to being overcast, he is startled to see his shadow and returns to his hole for six more weeks of sleep. Translation, six more weeks of winter.

Their ground hog is a rod puppet and the cup is the stage allowing students to act out the comical scenario of Groundhog Day. Through their playful performances, the students better understand and remember this legendary event in February.

The rod puppet groundhog emerges from his hole after a winter's slumber.

Materials:

- white paper coffee cup or styrene coffee cup
- drinking straw
- brown modeling clay, (walnut size) or 2" x 3" brown construction paper
- 3" square yellow construction paper
- 4" pipe cleaner
- cotton ball
- glue
- tape
- black permanent marker
- crayons or colored pencils
- small wiggle eyes, (optional)

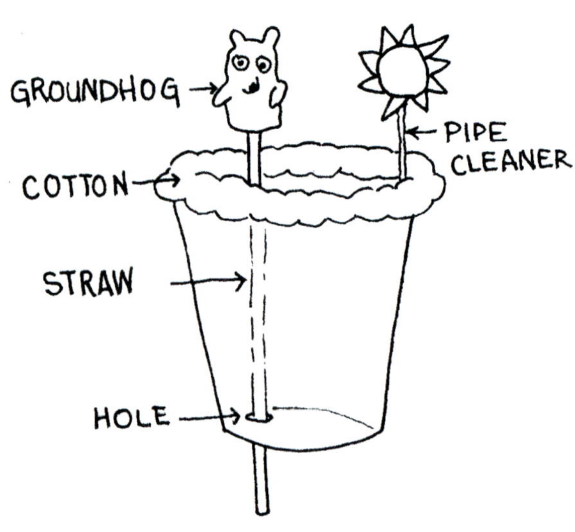

Procedures:

Before class, punch a hole in the center of the bottom of the white cup to insert the drinking straw, (a sharpened pencil works well). Also punch a hole near the rim of the cup for the pipe cleaner holding the sun.

1. Mold modeling clay over the drinking straw. Pinch on two small ears and nose. Press in wiggle eyes. Or, draw the groundhog on brown construction paper, cut out and tape to straw.

2. Imagine what the groundhog's hole home would include; bed, ladder, dresser, rug, pictures on the wall, etc. Draw these around the outside of the cup with the black marker then color.

3. Draw and cut out a sun. Tape one end of the pipe cleaner to the sun. Wrap the other end through the hole in the rim of the cup.

4. Glue cotton, (representing snow), to the rim of the cup.

5. Give a performance!

A bamboo skewer was used to add details to the clay puppet.

Cork board was used to create this groundhog puppet.

Reading Month Hand Puppets

Cat in the Hat, Dr. Seuss's mischievous character has become the mascot for Reading Month. In this month's long project, students first made a cat hand puppet and then a small book which they read to their puppet. While it was my intention for the puppets to be painted to look like Cat in the Hat, the students had other ideas which resulted in lovable, colorful cats.

Colorful, lovable hand puppets.

"If you want to learn something, teach it" or so the saying goes. What better way for students to learn to read than to teach reading to their puppet. Once the students had illustrated their tiny books with well known felines: Tony Tiger, Cat in the Hat, Hello Kitty and Pink Panther then lettered in their names, they read to their attentive puppets.

Materials:

- newspaper
- masking tape
- papier mache
- cereal box cardboard
- plastic containers
- craft glue
- pink felt
- black markers
- wiggle eyes
- wood base
- tempera paint
- brushes
- fabric

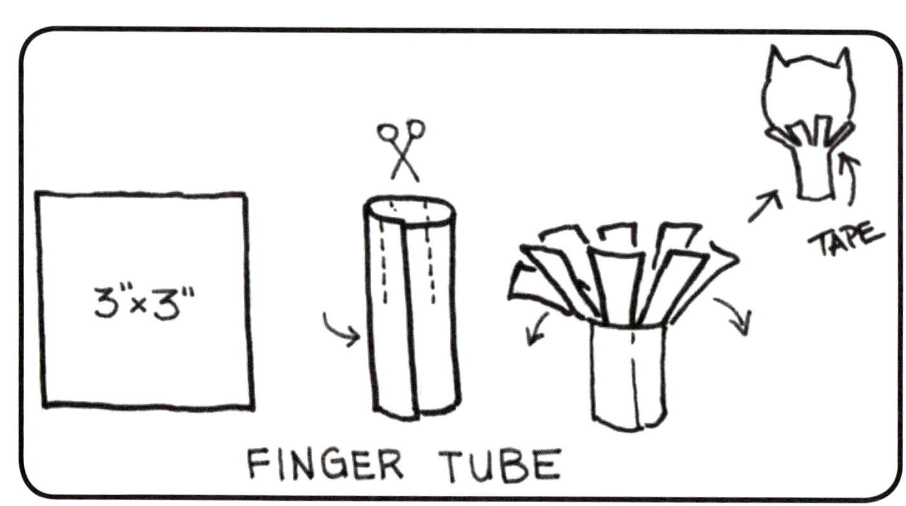

Procedures:

Before class, cut, glue and tape the 'finger tubes' and two triangular ears from the cereal box cardboard.

1. Wad one double piece of newspaper into a ball. Secure with masking tape.

2. Securely tape the finger tube and ears to the ball. Place on wood support with student's name.

3. Tear small strips of newspaper, approx. 1" x 3". Dip in paper mache, wipe off excess and cover head with 2 – 3 layers.

4. Paint with tempera.

5. Glue on wiggle eyes and small felt triangle nose. Draw in mouth with black marker.

6. I cut the cloth bodies in multiples using a rotary cutter on a cutting mat. Since I don't sew I glued the sides together with craft glue. When dry I glued them over the finger support.

A ball of newspaper, cardboard and masking tape formed the cat's head.

Kindergartners read to attentive puppets.

Milk Jug Hand Puppets

Some puppets take a degree of practice and dexterity to operate, not this one. Cut from a plastic gallon milk jug, these fish puppets easily swim throughout the classroom. Their translucency also makes them perfect to use behind a lighted screen for an impromptu shadow puppet play.

Holding the plastic handle of the milk jug makes for easy and immediate animation of the puppet.

Materials:

- plastic milk jug
- scissors
- permanent markers

As seen from behind a lit sheet, the fish became a swimming shadow puppet.

Procedures:

For early elementary I cut open the milk jugs and traced on the fish pattern. Even young students can cut the fish out with scissors because the plastic cuts easily. Mistakes in cutting? Pieces can be reattached with a stapler.

1. With good scissors cut through the spout and cut off the top.

2. Cut along the seam opposite the handle. Cut off the bottom.

3. Fold open the sides. Wipe dry. Draw fish on the plastic.

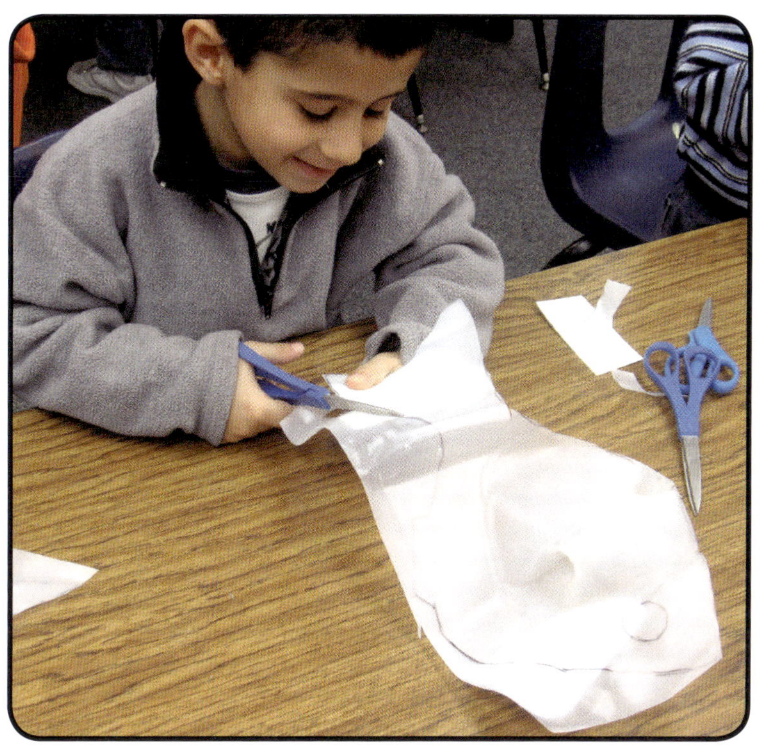

Students were able to easily cut through the plastic.

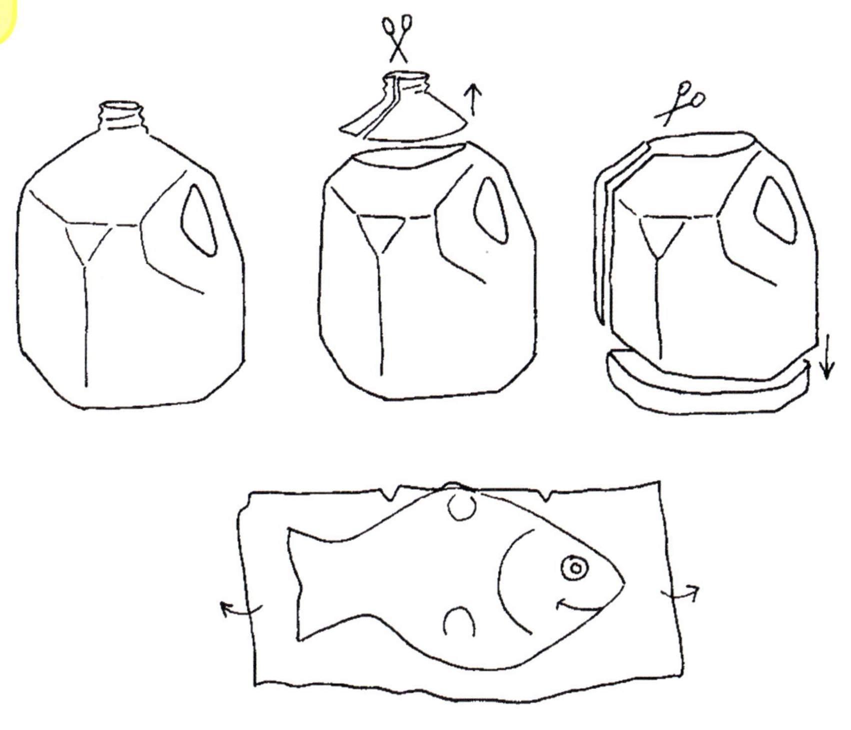

Extreme Art

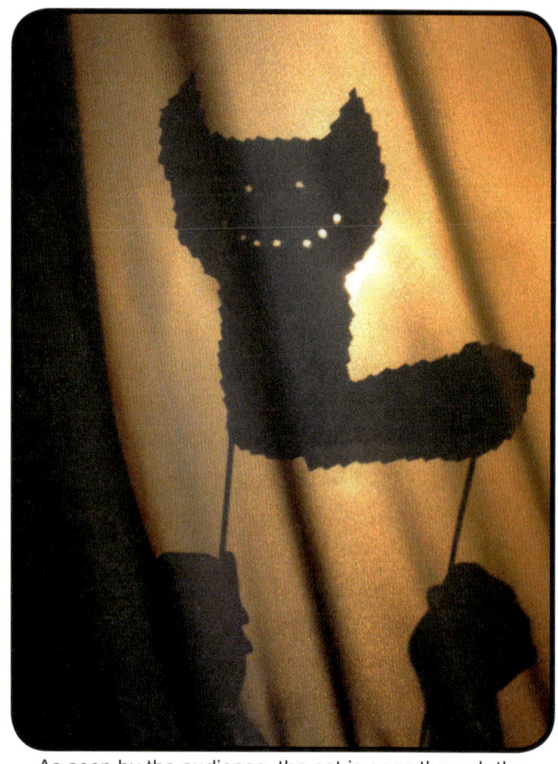

As seen by the audience, the cat is seen through the lighted bed sheet.

Shadow Puppets

Before there was the Multi-Plex, NetFlix or even television, families in Indonesia enjoyed epic adventures by watching shadow puppet plays. Rod puppets made from flattened leather came to life on a back lit screen. The puppets, perforated with holes to allow the light to penetrate, were accompanied with live music.

Shadow puppet plays are pretty much a thing of the past. But you can make this rich cultural art come alive. Hang a bed sheet from the ceiling, add a light source, and play some scary Halloween music and the classroom's atmosphere is transformed and perfect for making and performing shadow puppets.

Seen from the back of the screen, the student can move the cat's tail.

Materials:

- white bed sheet for a screen
- light source such as an overhead projector or clip-on style light
- Halloween music
- colored construction paper cut to 4" x 6"
- ¼" dowel rods or bamboo approx. 2' long
- pencils
- scissors, including the type that make fancy cuts
- hole punchers
- brass fasteners
- masking tape
- pipe cleaners

Procedures:

Screen

1. Hang a bed sheet from the ceiling, (binder clips work well).
2. Place a light source about 4’ behind the sheet.

Puppets

1. Draw then cut a simple Halloween image such as: Jack-o-lantern, ghost, bat, cat head.

2. Cut out eyes and mouth. A hole puncher may be used to add perforations.

3. Tape to a dowel rod and hold near the back of the screen.

4. Students may include a moving part such as a tail, wing or arm which is attached with a paper fastener. A second rod is taped on allowing the student to create an animated puppet.

A Jack-o-lantern and two ghost puppets move across the screen.

Like Indonesia, Turkey has a rich history of shadow puppets. I watched this hilarious play in Bursa.

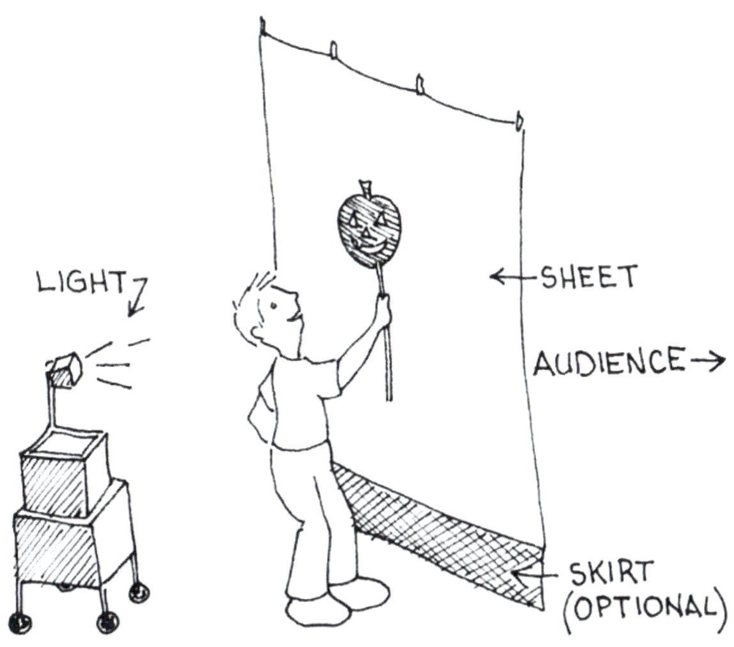

More than 300 butterflies created a peaceful tribute to Joshua.

Creating a Memorial

When a student, teacher or staff member dies, art has the ability to acknowledge the loss. Dealing with the topic of a death is difficult, but even young children need a way to respond. Making art provides a chance for dialogue and offers a type of closure.

Joshua died during the middle of fourth grade. Although it wasn't completely unexpected, he had Epidermolysis Bullosa, (EB) his death was still a shock. This disease is known as the Butterfly Disease because the skin is as sensitive as a butterfly's wings.

As a tribute, every student in the school created a butterfly. The butterflies, over 300, were hung in the hallway leading from the CI, (cognitively impaired) room to the fourth grade classroom where Joshua walked daily.

The colorful butterflies have made a fitting tribute to Joshua, who inspired everyone who knew him. There is a quietness that is created. The words Simonds principal, Rhonda Mienko, used adequately describes the project, "very peaceful".

Materials:

- wood clothes pins
- black chenille stems
- white tag board or card stock
- markers, crayons, colored pencils, etc.
- black spray paint
- craft glue
- sequins
- string
- pictures of butterflies

Procedures:

I spray painted the wood clothes pins black, drilled a hole in the head and cut and glued the chenille stems in for antennae. I also traced and cut the wing patterns, although students could have done this.

When the butterflies were finished, I drilled two holes through the body to thread string for hanging. Two holes instead of one allowed them to be hung horizontally creating a more natural look.

1. Markers or crayons were used to decorate the wings. Although the design may be real or imaginary, the wings should be symmetric. Both top and bottom of the paper wings should be colored.
2. Colorful sequins may be glued on.
3. Slide wings into wood clothes pin and glue.

A finished butterfly ready to hang.

Dots of glue and sequins added to the beauty of the butterflies.

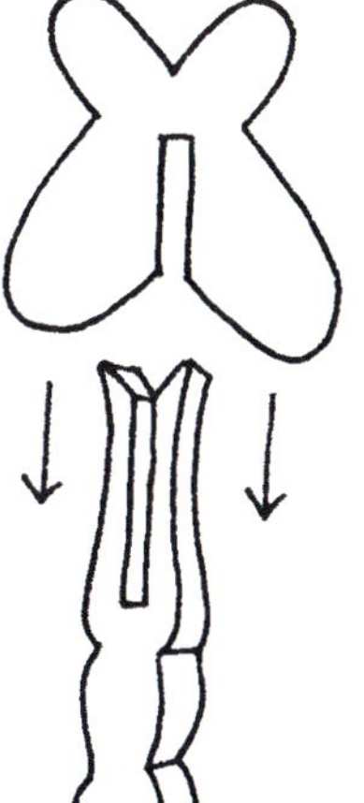

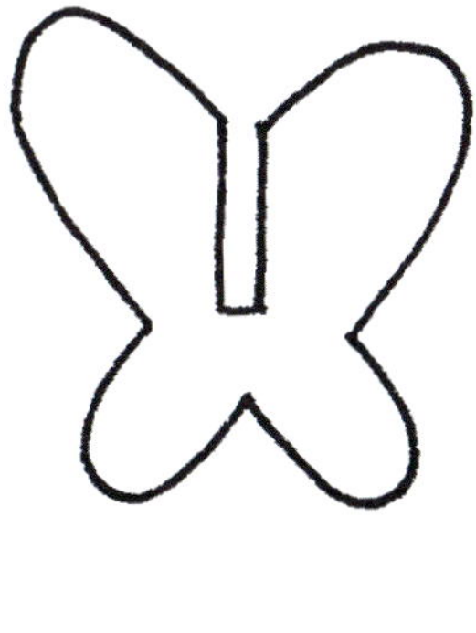

Increase 400%

The house is the place where young students have spent most of their life. What takes place in and around this dwelling is their world: family, toys, meals, pets and TV. While each home is different, it is this place and what happens in this place that has shaped much of their understanding and perceptions.

It would be wonderful if all children came from a loving two parent household, lived in a single-dwelling house surrounded by a white picket fence and had a cat and dog to play with in the yard. But this is the real world and it isn't so. Still, where a child lives is a big and influential part of their life. By interacting with students as they create art, as well as being perceptive to the art they create, may provide clues and an understanding about their lives outside of school. This can enable you to be a more sensitive teacher.

The theme 'house' can be developed in numerous directions. Consider houses in other countries, such as the mud houses of Africa. Consider memories of ESL students. Many of the families of students I teach have left their homes in other countries to come to America.

Architecture: are there historic homes or significant buildings near your school? Fantastic homes, castles and palaces were homes to royalty.

With clay stamps I created a title to glue onto the mural.

It Takes a Whole School Family to Educate a Child

A Lessenger School tradition began many years ago when a family art activity was connected with Curriculum Night. The parent attendance at Curriculum Night, (where parents learn about their child's grade level curriculum), had not met expectations and I suggested adding an art activity could be a big enticement. Although I have offered a variety of mediums over the years, it is a clay activity that the parents have repeatedly asked for.

Family art activities are unique in that they allow parents and children to either work separately or together on a project. It has been gratifying being able to offer a venue in which a parent or grandparent can sit next to their young child and both be engaged in the creative process of art making.

Over the years the art made by families has been saved and displayed at Lessenger. Parents, students and the Lessenger staff have enjoyed looking at the projects that they have participated in and now enhance the school's walls. This year's theme makes a visual statement to the importance of family involvement in a child's education.

Procedures:

Preparation is important for the family night activity because upwards to 200 people converge in the school cafeteria at once! Weeks ahead I began saving and cutting cardboard. I drove about the neighborhoods taking pictures of typical houses, including apartments and mobile homes which could be used as visuals. I also made sure I had the right colors of underglaze for the house project, (lots of a brick color as many of the houses around the school are brick).

- I sent a flier home with each student reminding them of the family art activity and encouraging them to sketch and color a picture of their house to bring in for the project.
- Using a slab roller I rolled and cut over 200 4" x 6" clay slabs. These were placed on the cardboard and stacked on pieces of plywood. The stacks were wrapped in plastic to prevent them from drying out.
- I made copies of the neighborhood house pictures and placed them on the work tables to use as visuals, for those that didn't bring in a sketch of their house.

1. With a pencil or clay tool draw your house on the clay slab. With a needle tool cut out the house. Extra clay is placed in a large plastic bag which can be re-used.

2. Draw/etch in the door, windows, siding or bricks, shingles, bushes, etc.

3. Paint on low-fire underglazes.

4. The painted houses, still on the cardboard, were placed on long tables set in the hallway to dry.

5. After the houses dried, about one week, I brushed a clear cover glaze over them and fired them in a kiln to cone 04.

6. I cut and painted sheets of ¾" plywood, (green grass with gray streets) to glue the houses to. I arranged smaller houses near the top, bigger near the bottom on the plywood panels to create a sense of perspective. I used Silicone in a caulking gun.

Note: The name of this project, "It Takes a Whole School Family to Educate a Child" is a take-off on the saying, "It Takes a Whole Village to Raise a Child" put forth by the Reggio Emilia approach to educating young children.

It Takes a Whole School Family to Educate a Child

Clay House Project – 7:20 – 8:00 P.M.
Curriculum Night – Thursday, September 8

1. Sketch your house or apartment in the space below. Look for **squares**, **rectangles**, **triangles**, **circles** and **semi-circles**. Are there other shapes you see?

2. Color your picture.

3. Bring this drawing to curriculum night to look at when we work in clay. Parents may want to take a photo of the house/apartment to bring.

See you Thursday – Mr. Hinshaw

I sent home a flier encouraging students to sketch their house.

Parents and children often work side-by-side yet independently.

Materials:

clay
underglazes
clay tools
brushes
cardboard, 5" x 7"
plastic containers

One of the many plywood panels of houses created at family night.

House Printing

Students love the process of printmaking. They love learning the process: drawing in foam, rolling the sticky ink onto it with a brayer, then laying a paper on top, rubbing over it and then pulling a print.

In the second class students added background to their prints with crayons.

Being able to repeat the whole messy process to make a second and third print is fascinating to them.

Materials:

- 4" x 6" piece of printing foam, (may be purchased or meat trays may be used)
- water base block printing ink
- brayers
- ¼" thick Plexiglas, 10" square approx. tape edges with masking tape
- 4" x 6" white paper to sketch on
- 9" x 12" white paper
- pencils
- scissors
- pictures of houses
- smocks

Students love 'mastering' the printmaking process.

Procedures:

1. Draw a house on the 4" x 6" white paper – practice. Redraw the house in the printing foam.
2. Cut out the house.
3. Place block printing ink onto the Plexiglas. Roll it smooth with the brayer. It should make a sound like kissing.
4. Roll the ink onto the foam house.
5. Place the 9" x 12" white paper over the inked foam and rub with fingertips. Pull the paper from the foam.
6. Repeat. Students will need to make more than one print to learn how much ink to use in order to create a good print.

Notes: Printing is always messy. Smocks, water, sponges and paper towels are advisable.

Extreme Art

House Printing

Numerous students could work at the same time on the long roll.

On a long roll of white paper I printed each of the students' foam houses. In the second class, they colored the sky, cut trees and bushes from construction paper and glued them on. Their individual houses collectively created an inviting community to visit or live in.

Family House Book

This little book has three unique features: its non-traditional shape, (shape book), the way the pages open, (accordion fold) and the method the illustrations are done, (thumbprints). These books can be displayed standing, open so all the pages can be viewed at once.

Accordion books can be stood up to display all the illustrations at once.

Materials:

- 5" x 6" poster board covers
- 4" x 18" white paper
- glue
- stamp pads, (washable ink preferable)
- colored pencils, thin tipped markers or crayons
- paper towels

Rectangular and square erasers were used to stamp the door and windows. It was the student's idea to use a handprint on the back cover.

Procedures:

Before class trace and cut two house covers for each student.

1. Tell the students they are going to make a book about their home and family. The covers of the book will be different from most books, it will be in the shape of a house. Show other examples of shape books you may have.

2. Demonstrate folding the pages. It is best to glue the pages to the cover before beginning the illustrations or students will begin on a page that will be glued to the cover.

3. Demonstrate how to create thumbprint people and pets.

4. Suggestions for the pages:
   - family
   - pets
   - friends
   - something I like to do outside
   - something I like to do inside

5. Encourage students to write what the illustrations show on each page.

6. Decorate/design the poster board house-shaped covers.

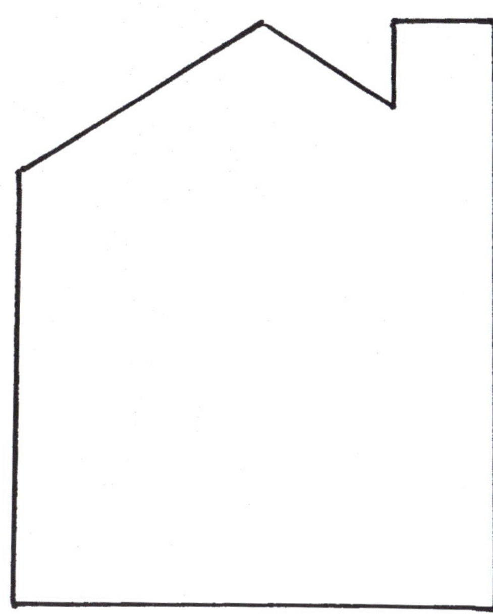

enlarge 200%

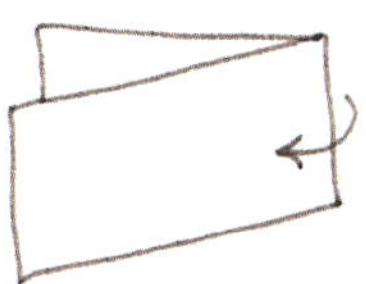

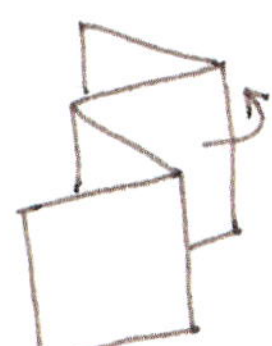

Two fingerprints create a figure.

Resources: Draw Thumb People and Draw Thumb Animals by Klutz Books
Ed Emberley's Great Thumbprint Drawing Book by Ed Emberley

Paper Houses

It's almost like a magic trick to learn to fold a flat 2-D piece of paper into a sculptural 3-D house. The houses have a lot of potential; one on top of the other makes a two story house, garage doors can be cut which open and close and houses arranged together create a whole community.

A winter scene was created in the school's display case by running white Christmas tree lights beneath the houses so they were lit from within.

Procedures:

1. Fold the 9" x 12" paper in half and open. Fold each side into the center crease and open. Repeat the process, folding the other way.
2. Open the paper to show sixteen creased rectangles. All the creases should be on the same side of the paper.
3. Cut the three crease lines on each 9" side.
4. Fold the paper into a house shape, folding and overlapping the cut ends. Glue down the ends.
5. Fold the 5" square in half to make a roof and glue in place. Cut doors and windows as desired.
6. The house can be colored with crayons or markers or decorated with cut paper.
7. Glue the house to the base and decorate further if desired.

Materials:

- 9" x 10" 80 lb. weight white paper
- 5" x 5" brown construction paper (roof)
- 9" x 12" construction paper base
- scissors
- glue
- markers or crayons

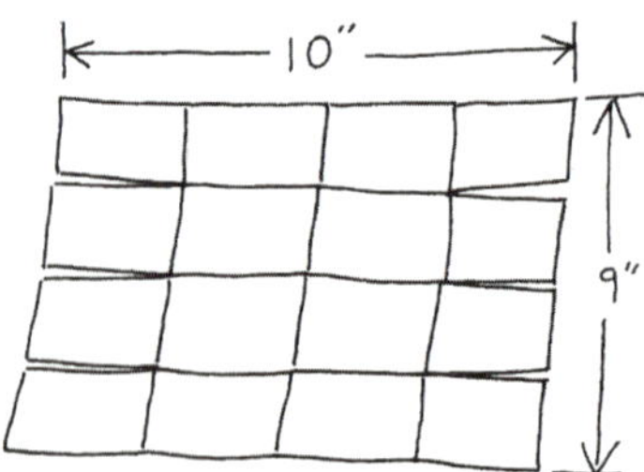

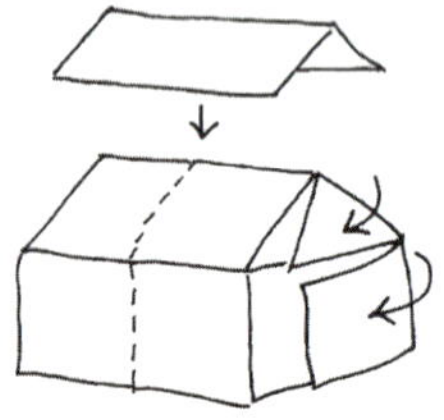

Clay Tile Houses

Drawing can be done on paper, but it can also be done on clay. Colorful ceramic tiles depicting a house and scenery can be made by drawing into a firm slab of clay which has been covered with underglazes. Once fired the lighter etched clay lines stand out in contrast to the darker underglazes.

The lighter color of the clay lines stand out from the darker underglazes.

Materials:

- clay slab 4" x 6"
- underglazes: blue, brown, green
- dull pencils or wood skewers
- clear cover glaze
- 4" x 6" paper
- cardboard pallet
- soft brush
- wire loop tool

Drawing on paper first lessens the chance of mistakes in the clay tile.

Procedures:

The night before, roll out slabs of clay and cut to 4" x 6". With a soft brush apply underglazes over the tile; blue on top, brown in middle and green at the bottom. Allow the clay and underglazes to dry to a leatherhard state; dry enough for the clay to be handled without distorting the shape of the slab. The underglaze should not come off when touched and the clay moist enough to be easily drawn into.

1. On the white paper draw a scene including a house, trees, clouds, etc.

2. Redraw the scene onto the clay tile: house in the brown underglaze, grass in the green and clouds in the sky, etc. Draw through the underglaze exposing the lighter clay beneath.

3. On the back of the tile in the center near the top, carve out a one inch long slot which will allow the tile to be hung on a nail. The teacher should do this using a wire loop tool.

4. Allow the tile to dry approximately one week. Brush a clear glaze over the top and fire to cone 04.

Extreme Art

The ceramic house doubles as a plant container and a candle holder.

Love Grows Here

Growing flower seeds in opened milk cartons on the window ledge and taking the 'harvest' home as a Mother's Day gift occurs throughout schools across the United States. Creating a flower container in the shape of a house, built large enough to hold the milk carton, completes the gift and will be kept and cherished long after the flower has died away. The cut windows, door, and open roof make the project double as both a candle holder and a plant container.

The edges of the slabs need to be scratched or scored and moistened to create a strong bond.

Materials:

- clay slabs rolled out and pre-cut
- clay
- cardboard pallet
- water to connect slabs
- clay tools
- glazes

Procedures:

Prior to class roll out and cut the five necessary pieces for the project. See template.

1. Demonstrate how to roughen the edges of the slabs where they connect to one another using a needle tool or toothpick. Moisten the roughened (scored) edges with water either with a finger or paint brush.

2. Firmly push the slabs together.
   Note: I check each house insuring the slabs are securely connected; often smearing a soft coil of clay on the inside seams.

3. Cut out a door and windows with a needle tool or toothpick.

4. Allow to dry then bisque fire.

5. Brush on glaze to cone 04.

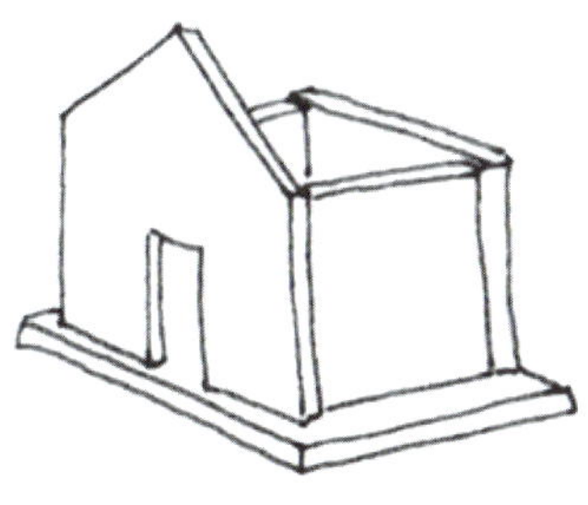

FRONT 3½x4½

BACK 3½x3½

SIDES-2 3x3½

BASE 4x4

Buckminster Fuller and Geodesic Domes

Buckminster Fuller was one of the most innovative thinkers of the 20th century. His most notable contribution was the invention of the geodesic dome. Fuller felt the dome had four advantages over traditional home construction: it could be built in a factory, it was lightweight, it could be easily moved, and it was based on the sphere rather than the cube. (Perhaps some of your students have been to Epcot Center and seen the huge geodesic sphere).

Students construct, evaluate and then often deconstruct and rebuild.

Constructing with packing peanuts and toothpicks is a three-dimensional spatial activity. As students explore the possibilities, some will create enclosed forms like the geodesic dome, some open forms like a stadium and others completely free-form.

Materials:

- foam packing peanuts
- toothpicks
- cardboard pallet, approx 9" square
- white glue

Procedures:

Before class, glue eight packing peanuts, evenly spaced, in a circle on the cardboard pallet. Allow to dry.

1. Show pictures of Fuller and his geodesic dome. Point out the geodesic dome is constructed from triangles; the strongest of architectural components. Demonstrate how the triangle form can be made using three peanuts and three toothpicks.

2. Allow the students time to construct and experiment building. Some students will construct the peanuts in a linear manner. Assist them by showing how making connections horizontally with toothpicks strengthen the structure.

3. For students who finish early, provide paper and pencils to draw their structure. People, scenery, etc. may be included in their drawing.

Fuller's geodesic dome as playground equipment.

A geodesic dome house built from Fuller's principles.

Extreme Art

A house with many windows; constructed with foam that had encased the school's new computers.

Fallingwater

Blocks of Styrofoam used as packing material lends itself to building large - large enough to create a structure students can 'inhabit'. The blocks are often molded in uniform modules which makes for easy constructing. Frilly end sandwich picks were used to connect the foam pieces. The wood picks were long enough to hold the pieces together while adding a little color to the whiteness.

Discarded foam pieces from a big box department store.

Pandemonium ensues if a whole class works on the structure at once. I had the building going on during the Buckminster Fuller lesson allowing about five students to build at once. Then a second group added to the structure or made changes they deemed necessary.

Frank Lloyd Wright was America's most famous architect and Fallingwater is Wright's most famous house he designed. I tell students it must be famous; how many houses have names?

The house, in rural Pennsylvania, has many of Wrights's most innovative designs. Areas of the house jut out into space without any apparent supports to hold them up, (cantilevers). A patio extends out over the waterfall. Not many houses have a river running beneath them!

Just as Wright did as a child, young students learn through the act of handling and constructing with wood blocks and materials.

As a young child Wright played with a set of wood blocks called Froebel Blocks. Later in life he attributed his greatness as an architect to his early years building with those shaped blocks.

Materials:

Class #1

- wood scraps, free for the taking from lumber companies or building sites
- 6" x 2" cardboard approximately (for cantilevers)
- white glue
- 8" square cardboard pallet
- masking tape

Class #2

- tempera paint
- brushes
- water containers

Procedures:

Show pictures of Frank Lloyd Wright and Fallingwater. Point out the cantilevers.

1. Allow the students some time to build with the wood and cardboard before handing out the glue. Encourage them to create a cantilever using the cardboard strip.

2. Have the students glue their construction together including the cantilevers.

3. In the second class have the students paint their houses. Suggest they paint a river flowing beneath the cantilevered cardboard.

Young architects envision a house with a river running through it.

We took students on a field trip to the Affleck House in Bloomfield Hills. The house was designed by Frank Lloyd Wright in 1940, slightly after Fallingwater and contains many of the same innovative features.

Dear Mr. Henshaw, 6/30/08

You had my son, Asher, in your pm Kindergarten art classes this year. The project you did on Wright's Fallingwater House made a huge impression on him. We were able to visit it last week and my older son (going into 2nd grade in another school) was especially impressed. I want to thank you for introducing us to this treasure. The arts are often given short shrift and you need to know how important your work is in helping children become reflective and appreciative of beauty.

Thank you - Alyce Howarth

Extreme Art - Fallingwater continued

Wood construction showing cantilevering, blue water flowing beneath it with pine cone trees and rocks.

Cantilevering can be understood by using a piece of cut cardboard held in place by a block of wood.

Frank Lloyd Wright, Fallingwater, 1935
Kaufmann House, Used with permission of Western Pennsylvania Conservancy. Fallingwater is located in Mill Run, Pennsylvania.

Resources:
Famous Buildings of Frank Lloyd Wright by Bruce LaFontaine, Dover Publications, Inc.
This book has coloring book pictures of Wright's buildings with descriptions.

The Dotty Wotty House

A large two story house painted with colorful polka dots. A house covered with stuffed toy animals. A vacant lot lined with rows of old vacuum cleaners. Welcome to Heidelberg Street, one of the poorest areas in Detroit. In the 1980's artist, Tyree Guyton began altering the neighborhood he grew up in.

Tyree Guyson, Dotty Wotty House
Heidelberg Project. Detroit, MI.
"protected property" of The Heidelberg Project under the U.S. Copyright Act of 1976.

Guyton's explanation for his inspiration for the Dotty Wotty house is two fold: his grandfather, who encouraged his art aspirations, loved colorful jelly beans and the world is filled with peoples of many colors. A portrait of Dr. Martin Luther King hangs on the front porch.

Guyton's art is controversial. Some even question if it is art or an eye-sore. Although the Heidelberg Project has received world-wide recognition, much of his work has been demolished by the city.

Materials:

- 12" x 18" white paper
- colorful paper circles and circle stickers
- glue
- markers or crayons
- 4" x 6" construction paper, (back door)

The house books are made by folding and cutting a 12" x 18" piece of paper.

Rooms of the students' houses are drawn and labeled on the inside pages.

Author with Tyree Guyton at Heidelberg Street.

The Heidelberg Project

On a field trip to the Detroit Institute of Arts we drove through the Heidelberg Project.

Resources:
www.heidelberg.org/images/stories/dottywottycomic.gif
The Heidelberg Project: A Street of Dreams by Linda McLean. A children's book about the Project.

Procedures:

Before class, fold and cut paper into house shaped books.

1. Show Dotty Wotty house. While most artists paint on a canvas, Tyree Guyton has chosen a house for his 'canvas'. In fact he has used the whole neighborhood including, trees, the street and vacant lots to create his art.

2. The students will be making a colorful house book. On the front of the book draw a door and windows then glue or draw colorful circles.

3. For the two inside pages, discuss with students what can be found in various rooms of their house: the kitchen, living room, bedroom, even bathroom. Draw rooms in their house. Encourage labeling or writing about the rooms.

4. For the back cover, glue along one edge of the construction paper door so it can open and close. Behind the door have the students draw themselves.

Building with Shapes

Squares, rectangles and triangles, the basic shapes of most houses, become the building blocks for construction paper homes. Torn paper grass contrasts with the rigid geometry. Markers are used to finish the artwork creating a residential area that looks welcoming and lived in.

Providing pre-cut shapes ensures all students will be successful and create great looking art.

Materials:

- 12" x 18" blue construction paper, (background piece)
- 4" construction paper squares, (house) plus smaller squares and rectangles for windows and doors.
- green construction paper for grass
- glue
- markers

Tearing the grass creates a nice contrast to the rigidity of the geometric shapes.

Pointing out the basic geometry of houses creates an awareness of the shapes found in most houses.

Procedures:

1. Show pictures of houses that display the geometry the students will be using. Point out the basic shapes and trace them with your finger.

2. Lay the green construction paper on the table or desk. While one hand holds the paper down and acts as a guide, the other hand slowly tears in a relatively straight line. Glue the "grass" to the bottom of the blue paper.

3. Have the students try different arrangements of the geometric shapes before gluing.

4. Glue doors and windows on.
   Note: Yellow windows indicate the lights are on in the house, blue reflects the sky meaning daytime, black shows nobody's home.

5. Finish details with markers.

Printed computer art

Computer Art Houses

Computer art at this young age? This is a good lesson to follow the Building with Shapes lesson. Using their construction paper house as a guide, have the students recreate it using a computer art program. Instead of gluing construction paper, the students will be drawing with light.

The students took their construction paper houses to the computer lab to use as reference.

Follow the same basic steps:

1. Using the pencil icon, draw the grass then fill in with the paint bucket.
2. Using the geometric shape icon, draw a square.
3. Use the straight line icon to add a triangle roof.
4. Finish details with the pencil icon.

Note:

A good elementary computer art program that is free: www.tuxpaint.com

A variety of building materials created a 'livable' city that is both colorful and fascinating.

Cities of the Future

Global warming may raise sea levels but this was not a reason for kindergartners to worry and wring their hands over. Instead they imagined and created futuristic floating cities. Solar panels, garden plots, housing and even schools were all considered as they constructed and floated their cities of tomorrow.

Materials:

- 1" thick ceiling foam cut to approx. 10" x 12" pieces, (available at building supply outlets).
- pipe cleaners (chenille stems), Bendy Wire, toothpicks, frilly sandwich picks
- foam packing peanuts
- 4" squares of colored craft foam
- plastic swimming pool or place to test floating cities

Procedures:

1. Fill a child's plastic swimming pool, preferably outside; although not a necessity. Discuss the current debate over global warming and how that could raise sea levels.

2. Show pictures of futuristic cities, (Google cities of the future).

3. Discuss and list sustainable elements a city or community needs: housing, sources of food, schools. As students construct ask them to imagine and include these, (the piece of craft foam may represent a garden plot).

4. Demonstrate building and constructing techniques. Toothpicks may be used as supports for raised levels of foam.

5. Test float their structures. Allow time to make revisions and/or additions.

On a warm spring day students took turns testing their floating futuristic cities.

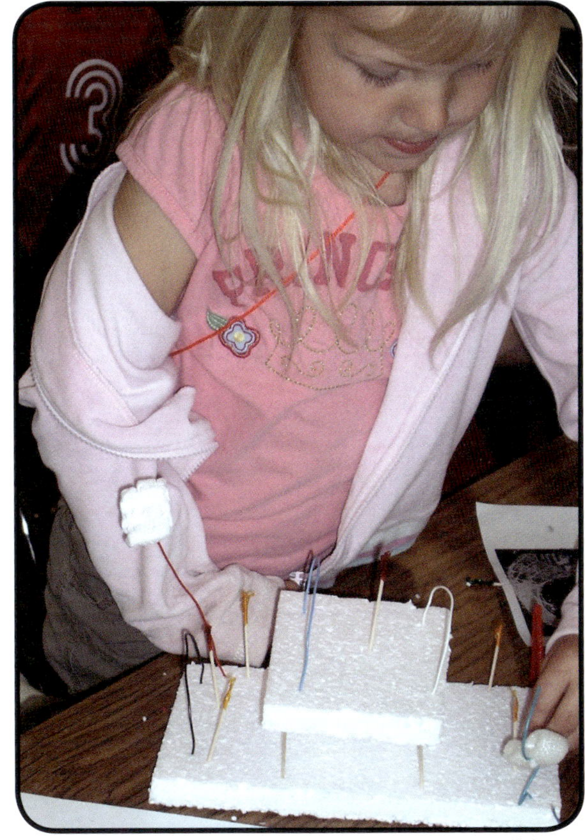

Constructing with foam provides an immediate, gratifying special activity.

Sun Catchers

Before Paul Gauguin came to live and paint with Vincent van Gogh, Vincent painted sunflowers on the walls of his house to cheer it up for his painter friend. It was with this idea that we created 'flower in a house' glass sun catchers. Kindergartners, first and second graders made these hopefully to cheer up someone's life that may be less fortunate.

Colored bits of glass fused to a piece of recycled window glass make a cheery sun catcher.

Even young children are aware of the economic hardships. With over half of the school's children receiving reduced school lunch, many feel the impact at home. But children are also eager to be part of the solution and understood that together we could raise enough money to make a difference. I offered the sun catchers for sale at our school board office and at the state and national art education convention, raising over $100 which we donated to a Michigan food bank.

Materials:

- clear glass, (I used discarded window glass donated from the hardware)
- colored glass, glass seed beads and glass stringers, available through craft stores or an art glass supplier
- high temperature wire, (I used Kemper 17 gauge wire)
- white glue
- plastic containers
- toothpicks
- needle nose pliers
- glass cutter
- fishing line

Making the sun catchers was like making a small collage using glass instead of paper.

Procedures:

Prior to the lesson, I collected discarded window glass from local hardware stores. Using a glass cutter, I cut the glass into approximately 3”squares. Next, score and break off the two top corners to form the roof. The extra triangles can be later glued on to reinforce the roof.

1. Show pictures of stained glass windows and tell the students that glass can be a form of art, just like drawing or painting. Also show the art of contemporary glass artist Dale Chihuly.

2. Place glue in plastic containers. With a toothpick place a small amount of glue in the center of the glass house and place a bead on it. This forms the center of the flower. Glue colored glass pieces around the bead forming the petals.
Note: The glue burns away in the kiln firing.

3. Colored glass seed beads may be glued around the perimeter of the house for added decoration.

4. A bent wire hanger is laid on the roof’s peak with a piece of glass or bead glued on top. This will permanently fuse the hanger to the house.

5. Place glass houses on a kiln shelf and fire to 1450 degrees. Note: Kiln shelf needs to be covered with kiln wash or the glass will stick to the shelf. After the firing, any kiln wash can be washed off the ornaments.

6. Tie fishing line or string through the wire hanger and hang in a window.

Dale Chihuly
American, b. 1941
Flint Institute of Arts Persian Chandelier
Blown glass, 2009
125 x 156 x 132 in.
Collection of the Flint Institute of Arts, Flint, Michigan; FIA Commission with funds donated by Claire and William S. White, the Charles Stewart Mott Foundation, and the Isabel Foundation, 2009.51

I proudly sold the students’ sun catchers at our state art convention.

A structure bigger than the students who constructed it.

Rolled Newspaper Structures

Buckminster Fuller's Geodesic Domes were all based on the triangle, which he knew to be a strong shape. Three rolled newspaper tubes taped together into a triangle create a strength that when combined with other triangles can create large and fantastic structures. The structures can even be constructed large enough for students to crawl inside.

This is a group project that will result in a structure bigger than the child. Students begin working separately rolling the tubes but once the structure begins taking shape they often jell into a team, deciding where to attach the triangles and resolving sagging issues. This is a great activity for developing a team spirit.

Materials:

- newspapers
- masking tape
- 3' long ¼" dowel rods
- Colored tissue paper, optional

Procedures:

1. Lay one opened double sheet of newspaper on the floor.
2. Place the dowel on one corner. Roll the dowel forward, rolling the newspaper over it. A tighter roll makes for a stronger tube.
3. Tape the newspaper. Slide out the dowel. Repeat.
4. Tape three of the paper tubes together into a triangle.
5. Begin taping the triangles together, first flat on the floor then raising them to stand. The strength of the triangle allows additional triangles to be added both horizontally and vertically.

Note: With young children I allow them to create free-form structures

Students needed a few tries to master the rolling technique.

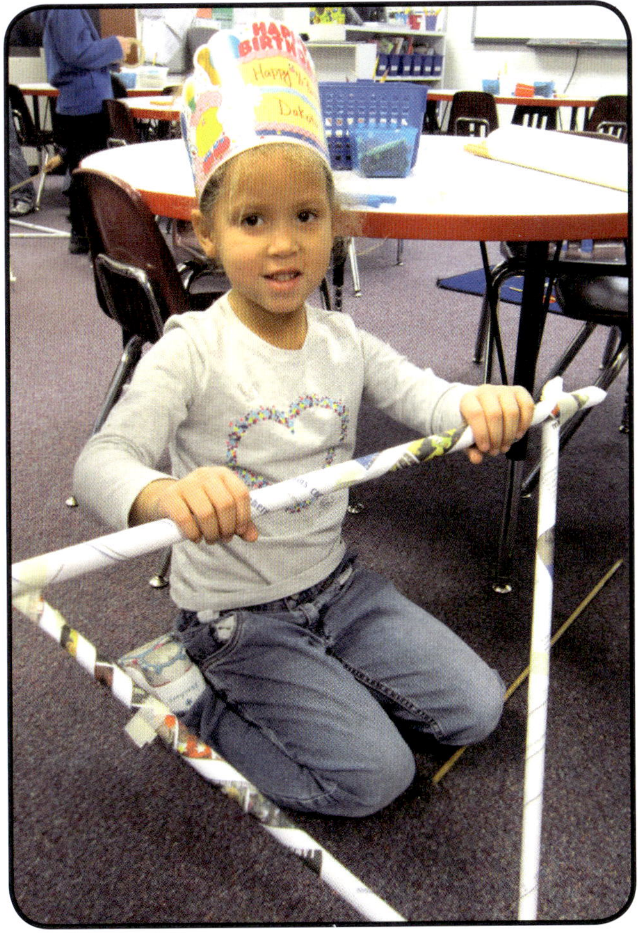

Three rolled tubes create a strong triangle.

People

The lessons in this section deal with the people that are central to a child's life: family, classmates and themselves. Family can mean anything from the traditional nucleus family which might include pets, to our global society. Entering school expands the child's circle of influential people to include classmates and teachers. Some of these new classmates will be friends throughout a lifetime. At this early age, self (egocentrism) predominates so it is only natural to include self-portrait projects in this section. Making art history connections are easy with these lessons because many artists have also studied their image in a mirror and made self portraits.

Edmonson's walls were lined with 310 cardboard leaders. This shows an active grouping of kindergartners.

Student Leaders

When Sharon Stephens, principal at Edmonson, asked if I could help the fifth graders make life-size cardboard cutouts depicting themselves as leaders, I not only agreed but suggested we do the whole school. Sharon was teaching the students about the importance of being a leader through Stephen R. Covey's book The Leader in Me.

When the massive project ended, 310 cardboard student leaders lined the halls of Edmonson, one for each of the kindergarten through fifth grade students. We planned the culmination to correspond with the school board meeting which met at Edmonson in January. To the surprise of the school board members and our school administrators, students also created a cutout of each of them.

Materials:

- sheet cardboard
- tempera paint
- large and small easel brushes
- plastic containers
- smocks
- razor type knife
- wood strips
- white glue

Working from photos, fourth and fifth graders painted the school board members and school administrators who exemplify leadership.

Procedures:

Preparation:

Searching the internet, I found a cardboard factory within reasonable driving distance and picked up the pieces in my pickup. I purchased 4' x 8' sheets for about $3.00 each. Two upper schoolers or three lower schoolers could fit on one sheet, so each student cutout cost a little over $1.00. The money for this project came from a variety of sources: a small grant, school funds and the art account.

1. The students laid on the cardboard as they imagined themselves as a leader. A leader of a football team might have his hand raised as if throwing a pass.

2. Upper schoolers worked in pairs tracing each other with a pencil. Teachers traced the pre-school through second graders.

3. The painting was done in three steps: 1. Select a skin tone and paint the face, neck, hands and arms and legs if a short sleeved shirt, short pants or dress is to be painted. 2. Paint the clothing, (as a leader), 3. Paint in the face, hair and other details. Note: As large as these were most students finished painting in one hour.

4. Using a razor knife I cut the figures out in my garage at home or at school.

5. Laying them face down, I glued a wood strip to the back which kept the cardboard from curling and allowed the figures to be stood against a wall. All the wood was free scrap from a lumber company.

6. The school writing team had each student write about leadership. Their writing was taped to the back of the cardboard figure.

On the back was glued a wood strip and the writing the student did about leadership. This kindergartner wrote, "I want to be a doctor because I want to make people feel better."

Razor knife used to cut out over 300 figures.

When it was warm students painted outside; when cold inside.

Children of the World

Most children around the world dress pretty much the same today. Still many cultures still honor their traditional dress; especially during holidays and festivals. Multi-cultural lessons allow students to learn about the differences but more importantly the commonalities we all share across the globe.

Materials:

- scissors
- 12" x 4" white paper
- large 8" circular coffee filters
- markers or crayons
- pencils or black markers
- glue
- 12" square black paper
- blue and green liquid watercolors
- eye droppers
- star stickers
- newspapers
- visuals showing ethnic clothing

Maasai children on the Serengeti

References:

People by Peter Spier
Children Just Like Me by Barnabas and A nabel Kindersley

Procedures:

This is a two session lesson. Session one is cutting the paper dolls and dyeing the coffee filter. Session two is designing/coloring the ethnic dolls, gluing the dyed filter and paper dolls to the black paper and sticking on stars.

Session One

1. Fold the white paper in half. Fold the top back to the fold line. Turn the paper over and fold the other side back to the fold line.
2. Draw the doll as shown. The arms and the bottom of the dress must touch the edges of the paper.
3. Cut through all four pieces of paper. Open. Turn two of the dolls into boys by cutting the dress to create the legs.
4. Wad the coffee filter into a ball. With the eye dropper, drip on blue and green liquid watercolors. Open flat to dry on newspapers.

Session Two

1. Draw and color ethnic clothing on the dolls. Each doll may represent a different culture.
2. Glue the dyed coffee filter to black paper. Glue the paper dolls to the coffee filter. Stick stars around the filter.

Learning to cut paper dolls is magical.

Visuals showing ethnic clothing is imperative.

A brother and sister in Oaxaca, Mexico dressed for a cultural celebration.

Children of the world.

Extreme Art

Murals can be more than just a pretty wall decoration; they can also carry a message.

A World of Friends - A Ribbon of Friendship

Seven colorful life-size students skip, jump and cartwheel across a thirty foot long wall. A red painted ribbon intertwines the students. On the ribbon are painted words supporting diversity: identity, cultures, togetherness, etc. Along the bottom of the mural is painted a green and blue Earth.

Hiller Elementary has a multi-ethnic student body where over thirty cultures are enrolled. Jen Cuminsky, Hiller's principal, asked if I could develop a project that would unite the whole school. It seemed only natural to paint a mural celebrating our diversity.

The year-long project ended with a dedication ceremony presented during a school board meeting at the school. The second graders sang "We Are the World" and ethnic foods were prepared and served by the students' parents.

Note: The materials for the mural were purchased through a small grant from our teachers' credit union.

Procedures:

1. Students laid on large pieces of butcher block paper, were traced around and cut out.

2. The paper cut outs were taped to the wall and traced with a pencil.

3. Our final arrangement ended up with seven figures so we used the seven colors of the rainbow to paint them. The colors would represent the multi-ethnic skin tones of children of the world and of Hiller.

4. Adding machine paper was taped to the wall and traced to create a meandering ribbon. This was painted red.

5. A large arc was drawn below the students and painted to represent the Earth.

6. With a small brush I lettered in the words of diversity. The words were suggested by students and staff.

7. Vinyl lettering, A World of Friends - A Ribbon of Friendship was commercially printed and added above the painting.

Paper figures were taped to the wall, rearranged and changed until a final composition was created.

Even kindergartners helped to paint the blue watery Earth.

Materials:

- acrylic paint,
  (We used the $2.00 sample colors available at The Home Depot).
- soft hair easel type brushes
- drop cloth
- step stool

Marisol and Big to Small

The lesson begins by asking students to consider how many people are in their family. Then they select that many pieces of wood which they arrange from big to small, representing the family members. Permanent markers were used to draw on the wood, finishing with crayons.

Dad, mom, sister and baby.

Marisol Escobar is an artist who became famous in the 1960's for making life size people from blocks of wood. She drew and painted the faces and clothes directly on the wood.

Materials:

- wood scraps gathered from the lumber company
- permanent black markers
- crayons
- white glue

Procedures:

1. Show pictures of Marisol's wood figures. Point out the way she left the wood in its blocky state and drew directly on the flat wood surfaces.
2. Have students count how many people are in their family and select one or two pieces of wood for each person.
3. Draw with permanent black marker, finish with crayons.
4. Arrange the family from big to small.

Students select two pieces of wood for each family member, head and body.

Some consider pets family members.

Marisol Escobar, Double Portrait of Henry Geldzahler,
Carved and painted wood, 1967
65 x 31¼ x 16½ in.
The Detroit Institute of Arts
Art © Marisol Escobar/Licensed by VAGA, New York, NY

Circus World

Alexander Calder is famous for creating the first mobiles. Before he invented the mobile he created a fantastic small circus shaped from pieces of wire, wood, cork and fabric. Calder made the figures: ringmaster, acrobats, lions, etc. so they could move or perform.

In that same creative playful attitude your students can also create small figures, people and animals. Through their imagination, bits of cardboard, wire and tissue paper, become small articulate figures. The figures displayed together can transform your bulletin board into an eye catching three ring circus.

Making a small movable figure is as entrancing to young children as it was to Alexander Calder.

Materials:

- corrugated cardboard cut into small pieces, various sizes approximately 1" x 2" (white cardboard is best)
- chenille stems (pipe cleaners)
- colored tissue paper cut to approximately 1" x 4"
- Wikki Stix
- buttons
- beads
- bendy wire
- colored yarn
- glue
- scissors
- fine tip markers

Procedures:

With a paper cutter cut pieces of cardboard. With wire cutters or scissors, cut chenille stems to 6" lengths. Cut sheets of colored tissue paper to 1" x 4" pieces.

1. Show Calder's Circus either with pictures or on YouTube.
2. Demonstrate pushing chenille stems through the holes in the corrugated cardboard holes, (see drawing). Glue is not necessary.
3. Draw in faces with markers.
4. Dresses can be made from tissue paper.

These figures blur the line between what is art and what is a toy.

Bending wire into a shape is a new experience.

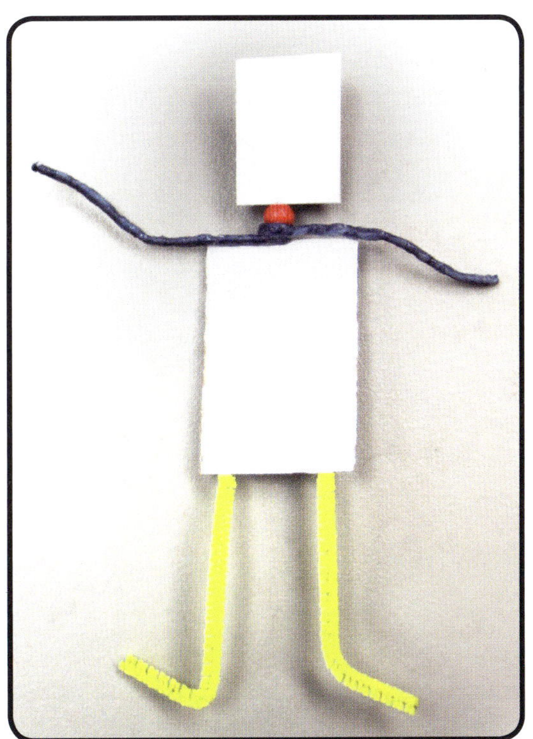

A figure is made by sliding the chenille stems into the holes in the cardboard. Glue is not necessary.

String Puppets-Marionettes

The complexity of making and operating a marionette makes them almost impractical for early elementary. But these small paper puppets with only one stick to hold onto are easy to make and simple to operate. They are a good introduction to this type of puppetry.

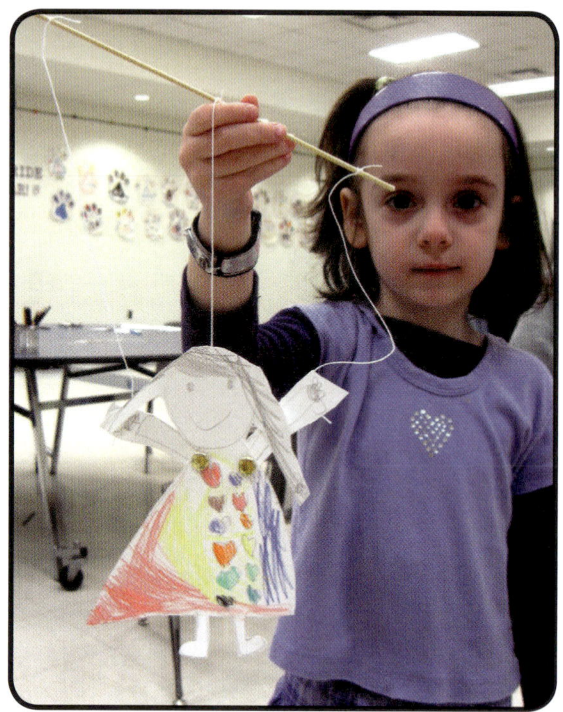

Self-portrait marionette.

Materials:

- 6" x 9" tagboard or card stock
- paper
- scissors
- colored pencils
- hole punchers
- brad fasteners
- bamboo skewers
- string
- tape

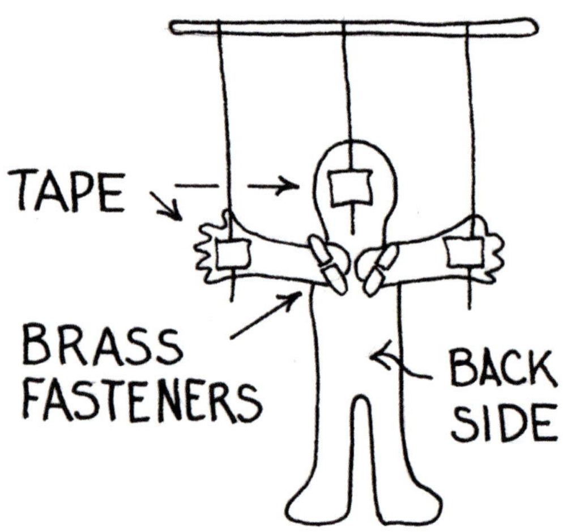

Procedures:

Prior to class, cut the pointed ends off the bamboo skewers. Cut and tie the three pieces of string to the skewer, one in the center and one on each end. Put a drop of glue on the end of the three tied ends of the string.

1. If you have a real marionette, demonstrate it or show pictures of some.
2. Draw a figure: body with head, and legs on the tagboard. Draw the arms separately, unconnected. The arms need to be longer than they really are because they will be attached behind the body. Note: Check to make sure the arms are large enough for the hole puncher.
3. Color then cut out.
4. Punch holes in the arms and at the shoulders. Attach with brad fasteners.
5. On the back of the puppet tape the strings to the hands and head.

The puppet is drawn on heavy paper with the arms separate.

Gluing a craft stick to the back of the puppet instead of attaching strings creates a rod puppet.

Extreme Art

The puppet operates using both hands. The toilet paper tube holds the body erect while the paper towel tube operates the hands.

Big String Puppets

Puppets come in all sizes, from small finger puppets to full-body Muppet type puppets. The puppets here are almost as large as the students. While the lesson shows students making self-portrait puppets, also consider animal characters from books or stories such as <u>The Three Bears</u> for puppet making.

Big string puppets are easier and more fun to operate than the smaller version in the previous lesson. They demand whole body/large muscle movement to operate, which is probably just what the “doctor ordered” for active energetic young students. As students practice operating them, don’t be surprised to see impromptu plays develop.

Note: Most of the materials used in the lesson are recycled making this lesson appropriate for Earth Day.

Materials:

- cereal box
- shirt cardboard or additional cereal boxes for hands and feet
- 2” wide ribbon; one piece 18” for arms and two pieces 9” long for legs
- toilet paper tube and paper towel tube
- markers
- scissors
- string
- hole puncher
- craft glue or hot glue

Procedures:

Prior to class, cut open one cereal box for each student. Cut off the sides. Draw and cut a large inverted "U" shape for the head (see photo).

As with most puppet lessons,I have my puppet introduce the lesson. This is a creative way to demonstrate the puppet's manipulation. Call attention to the materials they will use, recycling and reusing discarded materials.

1. With markers draw the puppet's face. Yarn may be used for hair. Color in clothes or use fabric scraps and glue.

2. Trace and cut out hands and feet on more pieces of cardboard.

3. On the back of the cereal box glue the 18" ribbon beneath the head, creating arms. Glue the hands to the ends of the ribbon. Glue the 9" ribbons at the bottom for the legs. Glue the feet on the ends of the ribbon.

4. Tie one end of a piece of string around the toilet paper tube. Glue the other end of the string to the head, allowing about 4" between head and tube.

5. Punch a hole in each end of a paper towel tube. Tie one end of a piece of string in the hole and glue the other end to the hand. Allow about 24" between hands and tube.

Student referring to a mirror when drawing a self-portrait.

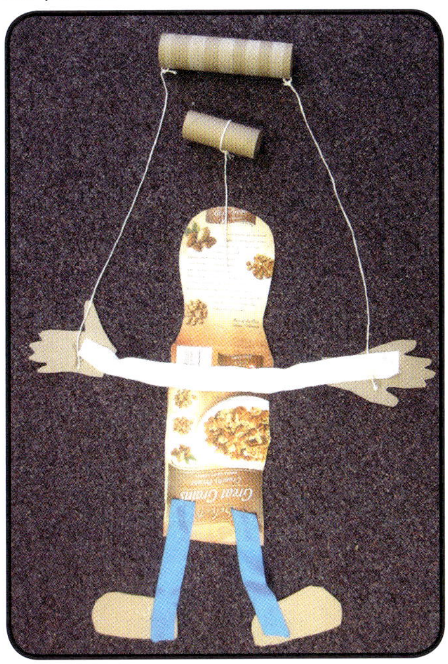

The back of the puppet.

Street performer with marionette in New Orleans.

Super Heroes and Beautiful Princesses

In the following two lessons, students first shape a small figure in aluminum foil and then imagine and draw a story developed around that figure.

Super heroes have special powers: amazing strength, the ability to fly or are even able to transform themselves. Princesses accentuate their natural beauty with beautiful dresses, long flowing hair and often reside in a castle.

Super hero with cape.

Materials:

- bagel aluminum foil sold in boxes of 100
- scissors
- colored tissue paper cut to 2" x 3"
- glue
- chenille stems cut to 3"

Procedures:

1. Show pictures of super heroes and princesses. Discuss the attributes of each.
2. Make two cuts along the top of the foil and one along the bottom, about 2" long.
3. Begin by gently squeezing the center or body of the foil together. Next gently squeeze together the arms, head and legs.
4. Clothing (capes, spandex pants and dresses) is made by cutting and wrapping the tissue. It is held in place with a drop of glue. Chenille stems are used for belts, dress straps, etc. The hair for the princesses can be made from a small piece of aluminum foil.

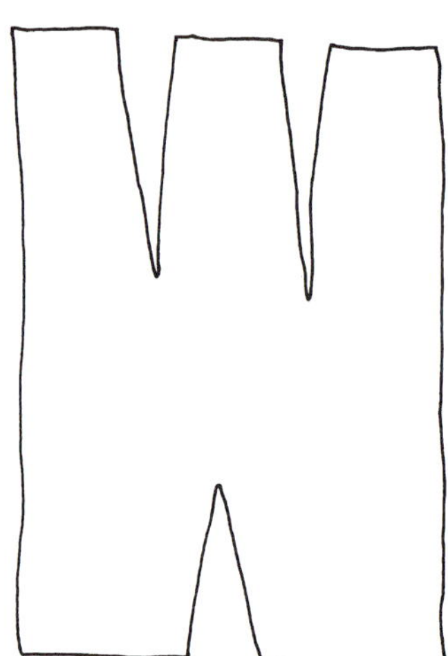

Storyboarding

All stories have five elements: characters, setting, time, problem and solution. The students' super hero or princess is the character. Where the action takes place, city or castle, is the setting. An arch villain or dragon could create a problem. How the problem is resolved, banishing the villain or killing the dragon, is the solution. For early elementary I don't deal with 'time'.

Even early elementary children can imagine and invent their own stories. Storyboarding helps them frame their story sequentially. Although they might not be able to write the script, they enjoy telling about the pictures and action. I drew a storyboard template adapted from current graphic novels.

While most kindergartners can't write their story, they can tell it.

Princess with dress and flowing hair.

Inukshuk

An Inukshuk is a figure constructed of large stones assembled by the Inuit of the Canadian Arctic. Inuksuit (plural) were originally meant as signposts which would stand out on the barren tundra landscape. They might call attention to a favored fishing or hunting spot or offer directions.

Kindergarten Inukshuk using a variety of interesting stones.

Students constructed small inuksuit from walnut-sized stones I purchased at a landscape center. Many found constructing a figure difficult and some opted for a simpler stacking arrangement. Once the students arrived at a satisfactory arrangement they glued it together with craft glue on a piece of wood.

Materials:

- a variety of rocks from a landscape center, (small flat slate works well for arms)
- wood base (approx. 3" x 6")
- craft glue

White craft glue held the Inukshuk together.

Extreme Art

A nearly life-size Inukshuk is a favorite spot for our courtyard bunny.

A Life - Size Inukshuk

In our sculpture garden (see p. 111), we constructed a nearly life-size (kindergarten) Inukshuk. The stones, again purchased from a landscape center, were so large and heavy the students had to work together just to move them. Once a satisfactory assemblage was made I glued it together with landscape adhesive using a caulking gun.

The kindergartners had to work together just to pick up the heavy stones.

Materials:

- stones purchased from a landscape center
- Note: cement landscape blocks were used for the legs. I selected flat slate for the arms.
- Landscape adhesive.

Fairies

A toothpick floss doll with paper wings, a bit of moss and a little imagination becomes a miniature, magical fairy garden. The addition of a painted rock lady bug and a clay snail and the tiny garden becomes a captivating world of fantasy. Children at this young age still have a sense of wonder about fairies.

The fairy was a simplified toothpick floss doll with glued on paper wings. I collected moss from nearby woods, interesting rocks and tiny pine cones. A glass marble glued to a golf tee for a gazing ball and pea gravel for walkways spurred the students' imaginations.

Toothpick floss doll fairy in her magical garden.

Floss Doll Fairy Materials:

- toothpicks
- 3/8" wood beads
- white glue
- wax paper
- colored floss
- fake silk flowers for skirts
- paper wings
- scissors
- colored pencils
- glitter pen, optional

Procedures:

1. Glue the toothpick doll together on wax paper which will peel away when the glue is dry. (I did this for the students the night before).
2. Place a drop of glue beneath the arms, attach a piece of floss and wrap the tummy area to the waist. Add another drop of glue to secure.
3. Remove the fake silk flower from the stem. Insert the legs through the flower and slide up to the waist for a skirt. Glue.
4. Place a drop of glue on the neck/shoulders. Attach a piece of floss and wrap the arms creating a blouse/cape. Add a drop of glue to secure.
5. Glue on hair using floss.
6. Draw in face with colored pencils.

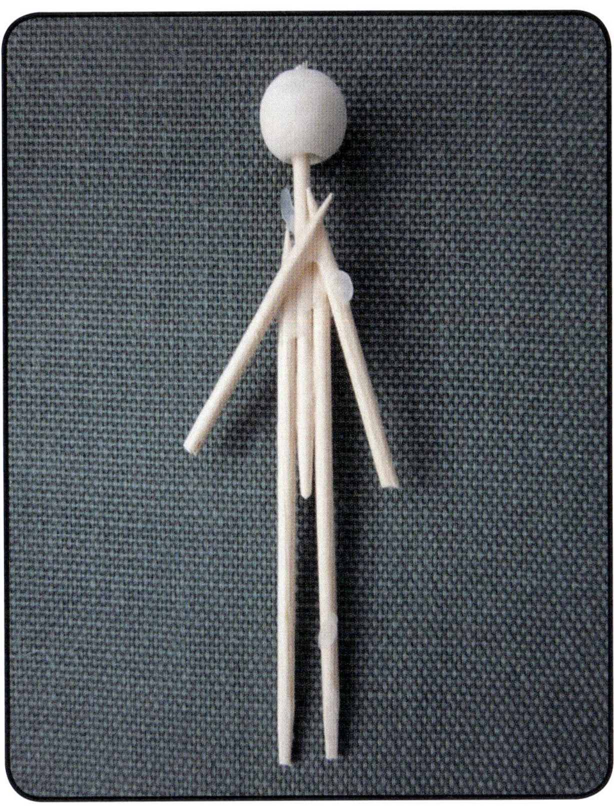

Glued toothpick doll using 4 toothpicks and a wood bead.

Fairy wings were based on butterfly or dragonfly wings.

Making the Fairy Garden

The students assembled their fairy gardens outside on a sunny May day. I set the 'ingredients' up like a smorgasbord, allowing students to select what they wanted to include. A note was sent home encouraging students to bring items from home to individualize their gardens.

Arranged garden with a white rock, crystal ball and shell water basin.

Here is a list of some of the items I had collected:

- I brought in three types of moss I had collected from Michigan woods.
- Potting soil and hand trowels.
- Clear glass marbles glued to golf tees (a gazing ball).
- Sea shells (for the fairy to wash in).
- Pea gravel (good for drainage under the potting soil and for making a pathway through the moss).
- Tiny pine cones (which appear as pine trees).
- Walnut-size white rocks gathered from a landscaped area.
- A bucket of water and can for applying water to garden.
- Magnifying glasses to examine the moss, which enlarged will appear as a forest.

Students assembled their magical gardens outside.

A once weedy courtyard transformed into a goldfish pond/sculpture garden.

A Goldfish Pond/ Sculpture Garden

When the Lamphere Schools began a kindergarten Chinese language program, the program was taught by Yingming Wu who is from China. Together we collaborated to have her students transform a weedy courtyard outside her classroom into a goldfish pond/sculpture garden (water gardens became popular in China during the Tang Dynasty). A $250 grant began the year long project with the purchase of a plastic pond, pond pump and heater. Throughout the year we continued to add to and develop our new environment: earth, wind, sky, and water.

From my home I brought fish, frogs, toads and even a turtle that students drew in sketchbooks they had made. They designed clay aquatic animal tiles that were used to make a small outdoor mural near the pond. We made stepping stones, creating an attractive pathway to keep spring mud off our shoes. Surrounding the pond we added clay frogs and a terracotta toad house. For the sky, students decorated a fish windsock and made wind chimes by pressing leaves in clay to add the dimension of sound.

Continued on next page

On April 22, Earth Day, we planted a small pine tree. The fish and a host of birds and squirrels are fed daily by students. During the second year, we added a bunny for the students to tend. Parents, enthused by the courtyard's transformation, have begun a school vegetable garden in the back half of the space.

The once unused courtyard has become a gathering place for parents and students; not to mention all the wildlife it attracts. Now in its fourth year the transformed space has been designated a National Wildlife Habitat Environment.

Kindergartners dug the hole for the pond before the ground froze for the winter.

The pond was purchased through a grant I wrote from our teachers' credit union.

A ceramic frog appears happy in his new found home.

Fabric crayons were used to decorate a fish wind sock.

Swinging Self Portraits

At recess the swings are seldom vacant. Young students sit. stand, lay and spin in them. Their close proximity to each other and distance from other playground equipment make them a good place to share with one another.

Self-portrait on a swing.

Materials:

- tagboard pattern
- scissors
- crayons or colored pencils
- poster board swing 2” x 6”
- string
- glue
- hole puncher
- mirrors

Procedures:

1. Before class cut the poster board swings and punch two holes in each end. I cut about twenty-five tagboard patterns, one for each student, to trace.
2. Have students trace the pattern on white paper.
3. Color and cut out.
4. Fold the figure at the waist and glue to swing. Thread one piece of string through each side of the swing. Fold and glue the hands around the string.

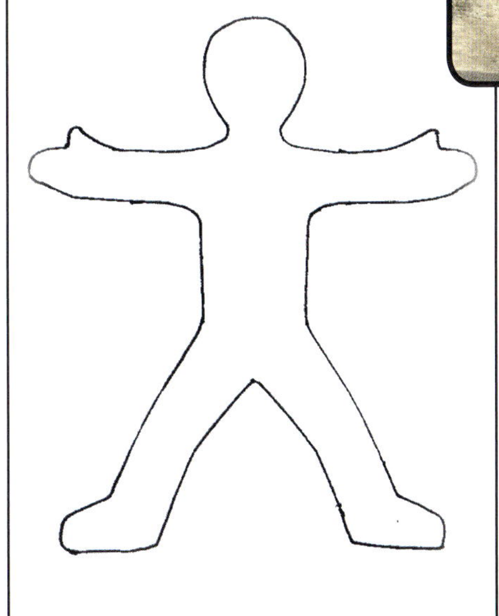

Increase 400%

Working from a Model

Artists benefit from working from a live model and so can young students. When using a student model point out the basic anatomy. Is the figure standing or seated? How do the elbows and knees bend? Look how one hand is raised above the head holding the flag.

It is difficult to make even a small clay figure stand so we made seated figures. Throughout the class I rotated the model giving every student a chance.

Even small clay figures are difficult to make standing up so we made seated figures.

Materials:

- clay: pottery, air dried or plasticine
- modeling tools
- wood block for seated figure
- flag pick
- glazes or paint

Kindergarten terracotta figures displayed in the school library.

Procedures:

1. Ask for a student volunteer to model. Tell them they must sit very still. Throughout the class, rotate models giving every student who wishes a chance to model.

2. Shape the body and head from one piece of clay. This will lessen the possibility of the head breaking off.

3. Shape the arms and legs; attach them to the body and bend at the elbow and knees. Add details including hair, facial features and perhaps clothing. Poke a hole in the hands to add a flag pick.

4. If pottery clay is used, it may be bisque fired and then glazed. Use mostly red, white and blue colors.

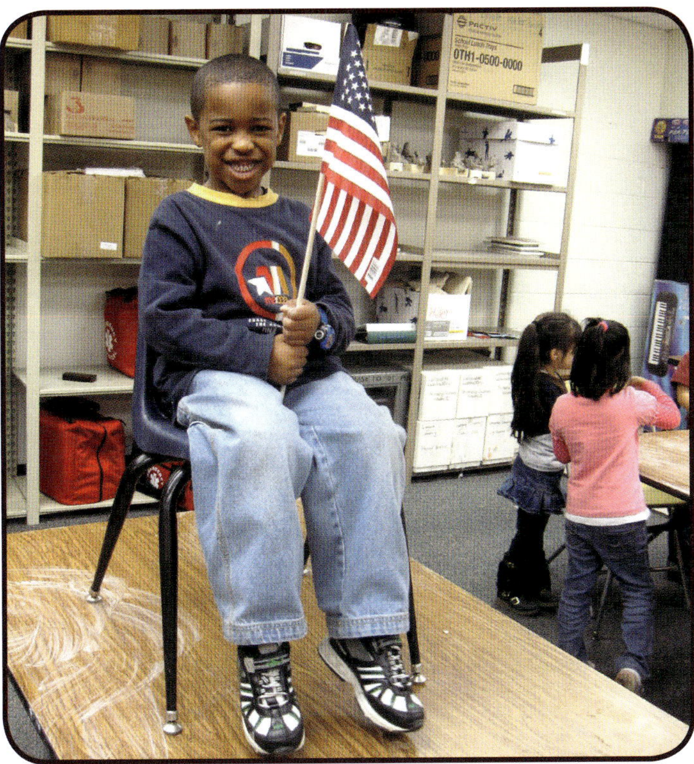

Students like the opportunity to be a model for the class.

Wood blocks were used while making the seated figure and later for display.

Twenty-nine smiling first graders on one small shirt.

Self-Portrait T-Shirts

Wearable art! Most children's art has a short life span, perhaps a few weeks displayed on the refrigerator at home. But decorated t-shirts can last years and often worn by younger siblings in later years. When I go into a classroom and a student is wearing one of the printed shirts I feel a sense of gratification and it makes all the extreme work on my end worth the effort.

Materials:

- black markers
- 9" x 12" white paper
- mirrors

Procedures:

1. Demonstrate the basics: heads are oval shaped and eyes are in the center of the head. Remind students we are only drawing the head, not the whole body.

2. Position the paper vertically. Draw a large oval then add the facial features, hair, neck and shoulders.

From drawings to shirts

1. To create a stencil that will fit on a young child's shirt, all the drawings and names need to be reduced small enough to fit on an 8½" x 11" paper. A copy machine can do the reducing. Some "doctoring up" may be necessary such as thin lines may need to be thickened or solid black areas cut away with a razor knife.

2. Once the layout is created it may be taken to a commercial printer to have the shirts printed or I purchased a small t-shirt press and 'burn' the stencil myself. This extra effort saves time and money but more importantly it allows me to help the students print their own shirt. I use a water base textile ink which works well but needs to be heat set with an iron once the ink is dry.

3. It is nice to print on new t-shirts. Perhaps the PTO would fund your project, but students can also bring their own shirt to school for the printing. I've done it both ways many times.

Black markers and mirrors are used to create the self-portrait.

I assist and supervise while allowing the students to pull the squeegee across the screen to print their own shirt.

Class Self-Portrait Banner

Replace the regular box of eight color crayons with a box of eight color fabric crayons, add a piece of fabric and a household iron and you'll have a beautiful eye-catching banner. Hang the banner of smiling faces outside your classroom to greet the students each day.

Save the banner until the students 'graduate' to middle school. Display again to create a nice reminder of the students' early years.

21 smiling faces grace the fabric banner hung outside the kindergarten classroom.

Materials:

- fabric crayons
- 9" x 12" white paper
- mirrors
- white fabric or bed sheet approx. 2½' x 4'
- household iron
- Two ½" dowel rods cut to 2½ feet in length
- fabric pen

Procedures:

1. Have students study their face in a mirror. Draw a large oval using either a skin tone fabric crayon or a black fabric crayon. Draw in eyes, nose and smiling mouth. Add neck, shoulders and hair.

2. Color skin. With a pencil write names on the papers.

Note: Encourage the students to apply pressure to the crayons. This is necessary in order to build enough of the wax onto the paper to transfer nicely to the fabric. For kindergarten I go over ones that need more wax.

Adult:

1. Cut around the faces. Lay them out, larger heads near the bottom and smaller near the top.

2. Measure the space to determine the size of fabric needed. Hem the edges. Allow a 2-inch hem along the top and bottom for a dowel rod to slide in.

3. Place the self-portraits face down on the fabric and iron on medium heat for about 1 minute.

4. With a fabric pen write the students' names next to their self-portraits.

Using fabric crayons allows the image to be transferred to fabric with the use of an iron.

I cut out and arranged the faces, larger near the bottom and smaller near the top.

The heat of the iron melts the wax into the fabric.

The self-portrait tiles were given as Mother's Day gifts.

Self - Portrait Clay Tiles

Andy Warhol used photographs of celebrities, screen printing them in high contrast with altered colors to create works of Pop Art. More recently Shepard Fairey printed a photo of Barak Obama in high contrast, changing the colors to blue and red, to make the now famous HOPE campaign poster.

You can turn your students into Pop Art celebrities in the following lessons. High contrast means low resolution, all the gray areas are removed leaving only black and white. The photograph is then printed using only black ink and the students creatively add the colors.

Materials:

- digital camera
- ink jet printer
- computer
- clay, light in color, not terracotta
- wood or cardboard pallets
- rolling pins or wood dowels
- mirrors, (second class)
- glazes

Procedures:

Using either a slab roller or a rolling pin, roll slabs of clay approximately 3/8" thick and cut into 5"x 7" tiles. Wrap the tiles in plastic until ready to use. The tiles need to retain their moisture in order to accept the ink from the print.

1. Take photographs of the students' faces. If possible use a white background.
2. On the computer, change the photos to high contrast and print to approximately 4" x 6".
3. Lay the print, ink side down, onto the clay slab. With a rolling pin roll the paper over the clay.
4. Lift one corner to see if the ink has transferred to the clay. Remove the paper.
5. Using a sharpened pencil, trace the image into the clay.
6. Allow to dry and bisque fire. Glaze.
7. Provide mirrors for students to use when glazing. Refire.

On the computer the photos were turned into high contrast and printed using an ink jet printer.

Cut pieces of wood curtain rods were used to roll over the paper, transferring the ink onto the clay.

The paper is peeled off.

The high contrast ink impression is traced into the clay with a pencil.

Mirrors were used when glazing to check eye and hair color.

Animation

It is hard to imagine a kindergartner that is not animated 24-7. But telling your students they will be making an animated movie is sure to arouse even more excitement in them if that is possible.

Fascination with animation dates back to a cave man that drew a running bison on a cave wall with eight legs creating the illusion of movement. Eadweard Muybridge's 19th century sequenced photographs of a running horse, Walt Disney's first full-length animated movie, Pinocchio, and recently Pixar Studio's mastery of computer animation have continued the technical march forward. Technology will continue to change but what won't is students' interest in creating their own animated movies.

Animation dovetails nicely with early elementary education's objectives: learning to sequence, working in a group, using technology and creating a project. While making an animated movie can be EXTREME, often taking weeks to complete, there are numerous fun projects which take only one class period.

One of the gifts of being a teacher is touching the future. Rick Shick took my animation class multiple times when he was ten years old in the late 70's. Rick recently won an Academy Award for the computer animation work he did for Spider-Man 2. His film credits include 'Men in Black III' and 'Harry Potter and the Sorcerer's Stone' just to name a few. In a speech Rick said my animation class was the only film class he ever took.

I begin the class by allowing students to flip through my collection of flip books which I've purchased over the years.

Flip Books

A flip book is a small note pad with a sequential drawing or photograph on each page. When held with one hand and flipped through with the other, the small images come to life: a short mini movie.

Post-It note pads are ideal for creating flip books. One pad of 100 pages can be separated into three books. The circular simplicity of a ladybug is a good image for a student's first flip book. Having the ladybug crawl across the pages, beginning on one side and ending on the other can be accomplished in ten to twelve drawings.

Note: Some very clever Post-It note flip books can be viewed by Googling Post-It note flip books.

Materials:

- Post-It note pads
- black fine tip markers
- red colored pencils
- masking tape

Procedures:

Before class separate the Post-It pads into three pads, approximately 30 pages in each. Wrap a piece of masking tape around the top creating a binding, securing the pages.

Demonstrate the process by drawing ten square boxes on the board or a large sheet of paper and number them 1 – 10. In box 10, (representing the last page of the note pad), draw only the ladybug's head along the lower right side. In box 9 draw half of the ladybug on the right side of the square. In box 8 draw the whole lady bug along the right side. Continue drawing the lady bug slowly moving across the squares until it disappears along the lower left side of box 1.

1. Lift all the pages of the Post-It note exposing the last page. Draw the ladybug's head along the lower right side.
2. Allow the second from the last page to fall over the last page. The drawing of the ladybug's head will show through. This allows you to know the position of the previous drawing. Now draw half of the ladybug's body along the right side of the paper.
3. Allow the next page to fall down. This time the drawing of half of the ladybug's body will show through. Draw the whole ladybug still along the right side of the page.
4. Continue this process until the ladybug moves across the pages and off the left side.
5. Color each ladybug with a red colored pencil.
6. Design a cover for your book with the title Ladybug, a drawing of the ladybug and your name.
7. The flip book may be lengthened by having the ladybug reappear and crawl back across the pages.

On page #5 the ladybug has crawled to the middle of the page.

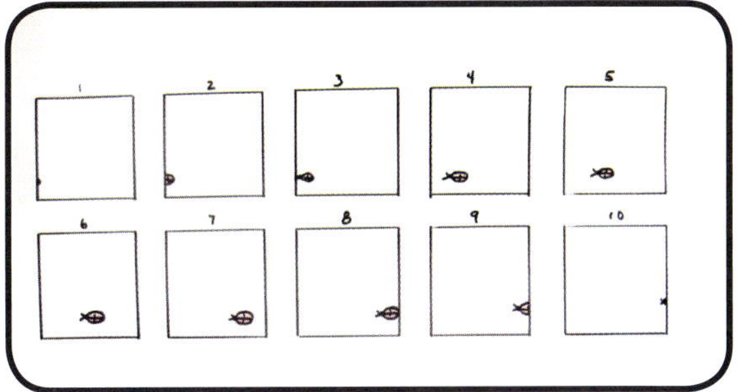

A visual aid showing the increments of the ladybug's sequence.

Things that Move

Animation is about things that move. The movement needs to be presented in a logical sequence in order to be understood. Thinking sequentially, which is a learned skill, is presented visually and mentally in this lesson.

Materials:

- white paper cut to 4" x 12"
- pencils
- markers or crayons

Courtney's bumble bee flies to the yellow flower.

Procedures:

Discuss with students things that move: fish swim, rockets lift-off, bees fly. Solicit ideas. Students will select only one thing to draw or 'animate'. That object will be drawn four times, once in each panel. In each panel the object will be in a different position, moving from bottom to top or left to right.

1. Fold the paper in half, then in half a second time. Unfold, having created four panels. Number the panels 1 – 4.

2. In panel 1 draw an object, such as a fish either at the bottom or the left side. In panel 2 draw the fish farther into the panel. In panel 3 about half way into the panel and panel 4 near the top or opposite side.

3. Color with crayons or markers.

A kindergarten student animating a porpoise jumping out of the ocean.

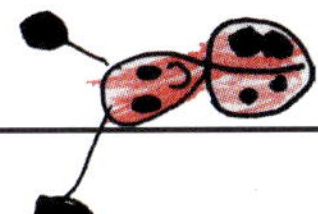

Drawing Animation Characters

Cartoon figures, because they need to be drawn repeatedly thousands of times to create an animation, are quite simple. Most can be drawn in a few simple steps. Children are intrigued to learn they can draw their favorite characters by following these drawing steps.

Materials:

- photo copies of "how to draw …"

Note: There are numerous "How to Draw …" books available or you can Google "How to Draw…"

- white paper
- pencils, erasers
- crayons or markers

Kindergarten rendition of Minnie and Mickey Mouse.

Procedures:

1. Draw the basic, underlying shape of the figure lightly. Note: Often students want to begin with the details, eyes and eyebrows, nose, etc. These are added last.

2. Draw in the larger details: arms, legs, fins, etc.

3. Finish with the smaller details.

4. Color.

Kindergartner drawing Nemo in four steps.

Catching Leprechauns

Irish legend says that if you catch a leprechaun he must give you his gold. Although kindergartners might not have caught the impish rascal; they certainly gave one a scare as it jumped in startled surprise.

A 99¢ green plastic hat helped turn the kindergartners into leprechauns.

Materials:

- tagboard or card stock cut to 3” x 4”
- 4” wood dowel or bamboo skewer or a pencil
- white glue or tape
- pencils
- fine tipped black marker
- colored pencils or crayons
- gold glitter (optional)

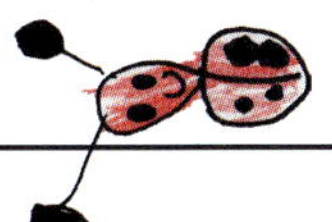

Procedures:

Prior to class cut the tagboard and glue a dowel about 2” into the card.

1. On one side, in pencil, draw a leprechaun standing; legs together, hands at its sides.
2. On the other side draw the leprechaun startled; legs spread, arms upraised, mouth open.
3. Outline the leprechaun with the black marker.
4. Color the leprechaun’s clothes green.
5. Twirl the dowel between your finger and thumb to create the illusion of a startled leprechaun.

Leprechaun standing; arms and legs down.

Leprechaun surprised; arms and legs up, hat flies up.

Twirling the animation toy makes the leprechaun appear to jump in surprise.

Kindergartners used a webcam connected to a laptop and used SAM Animation Program to record the action. White craft paper taped to the wall and table create a simple background that doesn't compete with the action.

Animation

Making an animated movie with children has never been easier. A laptop, webcam or digital camera and a user friendly kid animation program and you're up and running. I began teaching animation over thirty-five years ago using a tripod and a Super-8 movie camera that had a stop-action feature. In the mid-1980's I switched to a camcorder (providing instant feedback and ease of dubbing sound) with a time-lapse feature. Next I advanced to a digital camcorder. When I was awarded a grant from Palm and received fifty Palm handheld computers, the students made small, personal animations. Recently we have 'upgraded' to using a laptop with an animation program.

The magic of animation is surprisingly simple. An object, such as a coffee cup, is set on a table and one picture is taken with a stationary camera. Then the object is moved about one-half inch and a second picture is taken. This process is repeated over and over again, moving the object and recording the move. When the recording is watched, the coffee cup appears to move, becoming animated, by itself.

What will your animation be about? Some planning is essential. Here are strategies I've adopted over the years.

1. Dovetail the animation with the students' curriculum. Three kindergarten movies we made were: 'A-B-C Animal Animation' (the alphabet), 'A Numbers Game' (addition and subtraction) and 'Happy Town' (bullying).

2. Ask the students what they would like to make a movie about. Although this method is probably better with older students even kindergartners can have meaningful, creative input. I vetoed any themes that include violence.

3. Tell a story. The elements of a good story include characters, setting, a problem and a solution. These same components can apply to animation. KEEP IT SIMPLE. A long script can turn into months of filming and diminish interest of the students.

4. Show students how to make a storyboard. Even a simple storyboard can be an effective guide or outline to refer to throughout the recording sessions.

To see our animations go to: www.craighinshaw.com

For 'A-B-C Animal Animation' students shaped animals in plasticine clay.

Plywood provided a sturdy background set. Plasticine was used for the background.

A camcorder attached to a tripod was used as the student records a 'frame' using a remote control.

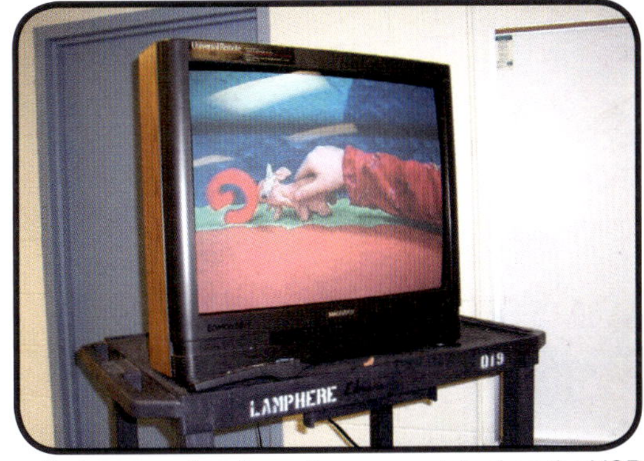

During recording the action was watched on the VCR monitor.

Components of Making an Animated Movie

Characters.
These may include drawn and cut paper (filmed from above with the camera on a tripod), plasticine (a favorite with students), or photographs (school photos or pictures cut from magazines).

Background Scenery.
Keep the backgrounds very simple so they don't compete with the characters. White butcher block paper is fine. If a background is made, such as a landscape or cityscape use colored construction paper rather than coloring with crayons or markers, again to keep it simple.

Title and Credits.
The movie needs a title, a 'the end' and credits. Credits include the students' first names, 'special thanks to' (this may include the school and you, their teacher). It is important for students to learn the importance of giving thanks. Computer programs allow titles to be made on the computer.

Adding Sound.
A sound track, music, or dialogue is added or dubbed onto the completed movie.

Colorful Wikki Stix were used to form self-portrait bodies for 'A Numbers Game'.

A school photo taped to a Wikki Stix body created the characters for 'A Numbers Game'.

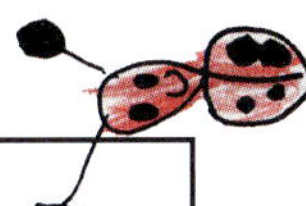

Once the Movie is Finished

It is time for a well deserved celebration of the completed animation. Have a premier showing. Invite parents, the principal, school board members, even the local newspaper. Serve popcorn and drinks. Make copies of the movie for each student. (I've had a parent volunteer do this).

The set for 'Happy Town' was created using painted milk cartons for the houses, pine cones for trees and scraps of wood for the cars and trucks.

Enter the animation in a children's film festival. I have often used the entry date for the Detroit Area Film and Video Festival as motivation to get the students' work completed. At the competition we have often won a Best of Show and gone to the Festival at the Detroit Institute of Arts theater to watch our movie on the big screen and receive our award.

Consider placing the students' animation on YouTube.

Suggested book: <u>The Klutz Book of Animation</u>. Purchase of this book will allow you to download free a user friendly computer animation program.

The milk cartons covered with papier mache and then painted formed the background for 'Happy Town'.

About the Author

Craig has dove on the Great Barrier Reef, skied in the Northern Rockies, jogged on the Serengeti, walked the Great Wall of China and climbed Mt. Fuji at night – all the while making connections and friendships with artists and art teachers.

After twenty-five years of teaching in public schools, Craig retired only to be hired back on a part-time basis. This has allowed him to do what he loves, teach and work with youth while providing more time for other passions: working in his clay studio, writing and traveling.

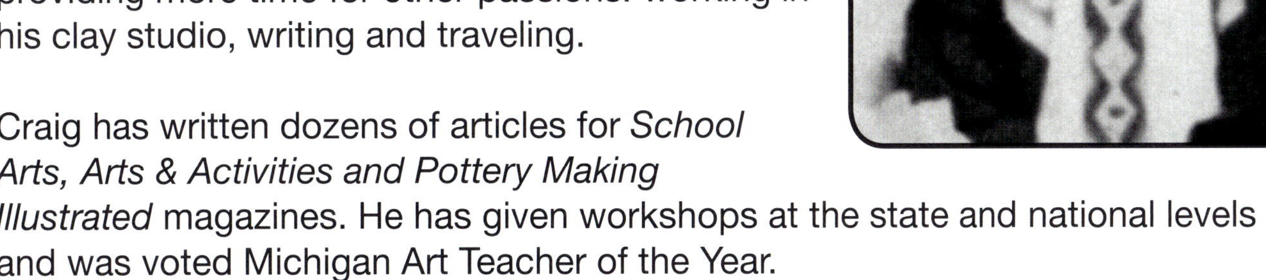

Craig has written dozens of articles for *School Arts, Arts & Activities and Pottery Making Illustrated* magazines. He has given workshops at the state and national levels and was voted Michigan Art Teacher of the Year.

Craig is married to his high school sweetheart, now a retired kindergarten teacher. He is the father of two married daughters.

Craig's first book, Clay Connections and his clay work can be seen on his website, www.craighinshaw.com